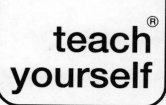

teach yourself

powerpoint 2003

moira stephen

GW00703476

powerpoint 2003

moira stephen

for over 60 years, more than
40 million people have learnt over
750 subjects the **teach yourself**
way, with impressive results.

be where you want to be
with **teach yourself**

For UK orders: please contact Bookpoint Ltd, 130 Milton Park, Abingdon, Oxon OX14 4SB. Telephone: +44 (0)/1235 827720. Fax: +44 (0)/1235 400454. Lines are open 09.00–18.00, Monday to Saturday, with a 24-hour message answering service. Details about our titles and how to order are available at www.teachyourself.co.uk.

For USA order enquiries: please contact McGraw-Hill Customer Services, PO Box 545, Blacklick, OH 43004-0545, USA. Telephone: 1-800-722-4726. Fax: 1-614-755-5645.

For Canada order enquiries: please contact McGraw-Hill Ryerson Ltd., 300 Water St, Whitby, Ontario L1N 9B6, Canada. Telephone: 905 430 5000. Fax: 905 430 5020.

Long renowned as the authoritative source for self-guided learning – with more than 30 million copies sold worldwide – the *Teach Yourself* series includes over 300 titles in the fields of languages, crafts, hobbies, business, computing and education.

British Library Cataloguing in Publication Data

A catalogue record for this title is available from The British Library.

Library of Congress Catalog Card Number: On file.

First published in UK 2004 by Hodder Headline, 338 Euston Road, London, NW1 3BH.

First published in US 2004 by Contemporary Books, A Division of The McGraw-Hill Companies, 1 Prudential Plaza, 130 East Randolph Street, Chicago, Illinois 60601 USA.

The 'Teach Yourself' name is a registered trade mark of Hodder & Stoughton Ltd.

Computer hardware and software brand names mentioned in this book are protected by their respective trademarks and are acknowledged.

Typeset by MacDesign, Southampton

Printed in Great Britain for Hodder & Stoughton Educational, a division of Hodder Headline, 338 Euston Road, London NW1 3BH by Cox & Wyman Ltd., Reading, Berkshire.

Papers used in this book are natural, renewable and recyclable products. They are made from wood grown in sustainable forests. The logging and manufacturing processes conform to the environmental regulations of the country of origin.

Impression number   10 9 8 7 6 5 4 3 2 1

Year   2008 2007 2006 2005 2004

contents

preface

Welcome to *Teach Yourself PowerPoint*.

Many of us need to make a presentation at some time in our lives. It might be a one-off presentation in a work situation or for an interview, or, if you work in marketing or training, you may give presentations regularly. If you are a student, part of your course could involve preparing and delivering a presentation. If you belong to a society or club, you may want to give a presentation on a topic of general interest to your members.

Whatever the occasion, if you need to give a presentation, this book will help you deliver your information with a punch!

You can prepare all the materials you need for your presentation in one PowerPoint file – the slides that you show to your audience, notes that you make to help you remember all that you wish to say, and handouts to give to your audience.

This book will show you how to create the slides, notes and handouts that you need. It will also suggest how you can add impact through the use of colour, graphics and special effects. Tips on how to prepare for and deliver the actual show are also provided.

PowerPoint is a powerful presentation graphics package – but don't let that put you off – it's really not too difficult!

I hope you enjoy using this book and find it useful when learning to use PowerPoint.

Moira Stephen
2004

01

getting started

In this chapter you will learn:

- what you need to run PowerPoint 2003
- how to install the software
- how to start PowerPoint
- about the PowerPoint screen and its tools
- how to use the Help system

Aims of this chapter

This chapter will introduce you to PowerPoint. We will start with an overview of the package, and move on to consider the hardware and software specification required to run it. We then move on to look at how you install the package on your computer. PowerPoint objects, starting PowerPoint, the working environment, online Help system and exiting PowerPoint will also be discussed.

1.1 Introducing PowerPoint

PowerPoint is a presentation graphics package. If you have to make presentations, it can help make your life easier by giving you the tools you need to produce your own materials with little or no help from presentation graphics specialists.

You can use PowerPoint to produce:

Slides

Slides are the individual pages of your presentation. They may contain text, graphs, clip art, tables, drawings, animation, movies, music, shapes – and more! PowerPoint will allow you to present your slides via a slide show on your computer, 35mm slides or overhead projector transparencies.

Speaker's Notes

A speaker's notes page accompanies each slide you create. Each notes page contains a small image of the slide plus any notes you type in. You can print the pages and use them to prompt you during your presentation.

Handouts

Handouts consist of smaller, printed versions of your slides that can be printed 1, 2, 3, 4, 6 or 9 slides to a page. They provide useful backup material for your audience and can easily be customized with your company name or logo.

Outline

A presentation Outline contains the slide titles and main text items, but neither art nor text added by using the text tool. The Outline gives a useful overview of your presentation's structure.

◆ A PowerPoint presentation is a collection of slides, with optional, but useful support materials, speaker's notes, handouts and an outline, all in one file.

1.2 Hardware and software requirements

The hardware and software specifications given are for Office 2003. The recommended configuration is a PC with Windows 2000 or XP, a Pentium III processor and 128 MB of RAM.

The minimum specification is:

Processor	133 MHz or higher; Pentium III recommended
Operating system	Windows 2000 with Service Pack 3, Windows XP, or a later system
RAM	64 MB (128 MB recommended) for the operating system, plus 8 MB for each program running simultaneously
Hard disk	Approximately 245 MB in total, with 115 MB on the hard disk where the operating system is installed.
CD-ROM drive	
Monitor	Super VGA or higher-resolution
Mouse	Microsoft Mouse, IntelliMouse® or compatible pointing device

See **http://www.microsoft.com/uk/office/preview/sysreq.asp** for full details of system requirements.

1.3 Installing PowerPoint 2003

PowerPoint is supplied in all the Office suite editions except for the Basic one. For full details of what is included in each edition visit **http://www.microsoft.com/uk/office/preview/editions.asp**

To install Microsoft Office, follow the on-screen instructions.

1 Insert the CD into the CD drive.

• The CD will launch automatically, and the setup begin.

2 At the **Setup** dialog box, enter the 25-character product key.

3 For the user information, enter your name, initials (optional) and organization (optional).

• Your name will be used in the Author box in the Properties dialog box in the Office programs.

4 Read the End-User License Agreement and select *I accept the terms …* (if you don't agree, you can't continue!).

5 Select the type of installation.

6 At the final Setup stage, select the options and you're done!

Activate your software

The first time that you open an Office application you will be prompted to activate your software. If you don't activate it, you can open the applications a total of 50 times, then many of the features become inactive. Activation verifies the legitimacy of your license and discourages software piracy.

It's very easy to do – just follow the prompts and activate it online – it takes 2 seconds!

1.4 PowerPoint objects

In PowerPoint you work with *objects*. These may be:

• Text   • Drawings   • Graphs

• Clip art   • Movies   • Sounds

• Tables   • Organization charts

You'll learn how to create and manipulate these objects as you work with the package.

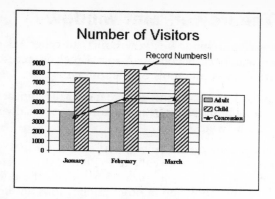

1.5 Starting PowerPoint

From the Start menu:

1 Click the **Start** button on the Task Bar.

2 Point to **All Programs**.

3 Point to **Microsoft Office**.

4 Click **Microsoft Office PowerPoint 2003**.

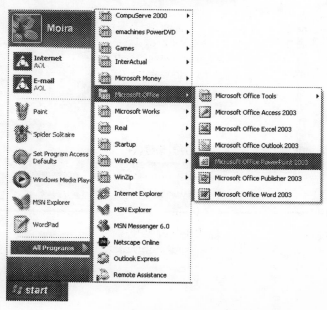

1.6 The PowerPoint window

The PowerPoint window is very similar to other Microsoft application windows. If you use Word, Excel or Access you will recognize some of the tools on the toolbars.

The Standard and Formatting toolbars usually appear along the top of the window. The Drawing toolbar is usually along the bottom of the window.

We'll take a tour of the PowerPoint screen, so that you know what the various areas are called. You'll find the different screen areas referred to by their 'proper' names in the online Help, throughout this book and in other publications on the package.

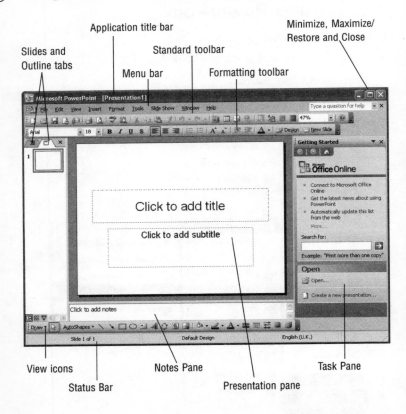

Application title bar

Standard toolbar

Minimize, Maximize/ Restore and Close

Slides and Outline tabs

Menu bar

Formatting toolbar

View icons

Notes Pane

Task Pane

Status Bar

Presentation pane

Menus and toolbars

Office applications personalize your menus and toolbars automatically. The items that you use most often are featured on your personalized toolbars or menus.

Once you start using PowerPoint, you'll find that the menu options most recently used will be displayed first when you open a menu (this is your personalized menu). You can expand the menus to reveal all commands (simply click on the down arrow that appears at the bottom of each menu). You may find that the menu automatically expands if you just wait once you've opened it. If you wish to modify the way that the menus work, open the **View** menu and choose **Toolbars, Customize**.

The Standard and Formatting toolbars share a single row, so that you have more room for your work. You can disable this option from the **Options** tab, or you can toggle the option by clicking the drop-down arrow at the end of either the Standard or Formatting toolbar and selecting **Show Buttons on One Row** or **Show Buttons on Two Rows** as required.

Don't panic if your toolbars and menus are not exactly the same as those in this book. Variations will occur depending upon the options you have set.

1.7 Menus

There are nine main menus in your PowerPoint application window. You can use these menus to access any function or feature available in PowerPoint. I suggest you have a browse through them to get an idea of what's available – some menu items on the lists may appear familiar to you, some will be new.

You can display a menu and select menu options using the mouse or the keyboard.

Using the mouse

1 Click on the menu name to display the list of options available in that menu.

2 Click on the menu item you wish to use.

• Click the extension arrow at the bottom of your personalized menu to display all the options available.

Using the keyboard

Each menu name has one character underlined.

To open a menu:

• Hold down the [**Alt**] key and press the underlined letter e.g. [**Alt**]-[**F**] for the **File** menu, [**Alt**]-[**I**] for the **Insert** menu.

Each item in a menu list also has a letter underlined in it. To select an item from the menu list either:

• Press the appropriate letter, or

• Use the up and down arrow keys on your keyboard until the item you want is selected, then press [**Enter**].

Once a menu list is displayed, you can press the right or left arrow keys to move from one menu to another.

To close a menu without selecting an item from the list:

• Click the menu name again, click anywhere off the menu list or press [**Esc**].

In addition to the menus, many commands can be initiated using the toolbars, keyboard shortcuts or shortcut menus. Each of these areas will be covered as you progress through the book.

1.8 Help!

As you work with PowerPoint you will most probably find that you come a bit unstuck from time to time and need help! There are several ways to get help – most very intuitive and user friendly.

Type a question for help box

You can access the Help system using the *Type a question for help* box on the Menu bar.

1 Type your question.

how do I create a slide

2 Press [**Enter**].

3 Choose a Help topic from the Search Results Task Pane that is displayed – click on it.

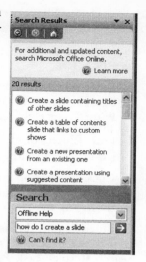

PowerPoint Help Task Pane

To show the PowerPoint Help Task Pane:

+ Click the PowerPoint Help tool on the Standard toolbar.

Or

+ Press **[F1]**.

The Task Pane has three main areas:

+ The Offline Help can be accessed from the **Search for:** field and the **Table of Contents** option in the top area.

+ The Online Help can be accessed from the middle area.

+ Topics like 'What's New', 'Contact Us' and 'Accessibility Help' can be accessed from the **See also** list at the bottom of the Task Pane.

The Back , Forward and Home icons at the top of a Task Pane take you backwards and forwards through the topics that you have used recently, or Home to the Getting Started Task Pane that appears when you open the application.

Search for

1 Enter a keyword or keywords in the **Search for:** field at the top of the PowerPoint Help Task Pane.

2 Press [Enter] or click ▣ to display a list of topics on the subject.

3 Click on the topic that sounds most likely in the Search Results Task Pane to display the Help page.

If you can't find the help that you need, click *Can't find it?* at the bottom of the Search Results Task Pane – PowerPoint will suggest how you could make your search more successful.

You can also search another location in the **Search** options at the bottom of the Task Pane, or try different keywords.

Table of Contents

You can browse through the Help with this option.

1 Click 🕮 Table of Contents near the top of the Task Pane.

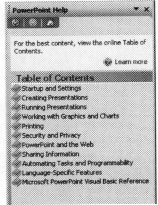

2 Click on a book in the table of contents list – the book will open to display other books or topics that may interest you.

• You can adjust the width of the Table of Contents pane by dragging the left edge of it.

3 Open another book, or click on a topic to display the Help page on that topic.

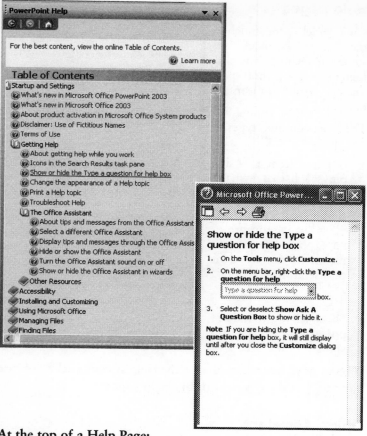

At the top of a Help Page:

⊞   Tiles the Help Task Pane and the Help page.

▥   Un-tiles the Help Task Pane and the Help page.

⇦   Takes you back through the Help pages viewed.

⇨   Takes you forward through the Help pages viewed.

🖨   Prints the Help page.

Help pages

On any Help page, much of the text will be black, but some will be blue. The blue text indicates a 'hot spot' that can display some information.

The most common types of hot spots are:

* Bulleted item ▶ – displays a list of instructions.

* Embedded item – displays (usually in green) an explanation or definition of the word or phrase attached to it.

* Tip – suggested Help.

* Show All – expands or collapses all the hot spots on the page.

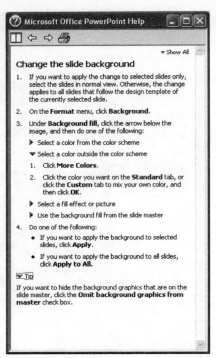

When you've finished exploring the Help system, click the **Close** button ⊠ at the top right of the Help window.

Office Assistant

You can use the Assistant as a 'front end' to the Help system.

1 Open the **Help** menu and choose **Show Office Assistant**.

2 Click on the Office Assistant to display the dialog bubble.

3 Type in your question.

4 Click **Search**.

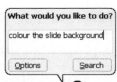

The Search Results Task Pane will be displayed – click on a topic to display the Help page.

To customize the Office Assistant

You can customize the Office Assistant to take on a different appearance, or behave in a different way.

1 Click the **Office Assistant**.

2 Click the **Options** button.

3 To change its appearance, select the **Gallery** tab and browse through the options (use the **Next** and **Back** buttons to move through the various guises).

♦ If you find an Assistant you would like to use, click **OK**.

♦ To leave the Assistant as it was, click **Cancel**.

4 To change its behaviour, select the **Options** tab, select or deselect the options as required – click to switch them on or off. A tick in a box means an option is selected.

♦ If you don't want to use the Assistant, you can switch it off on the **Options** tab – simply deselect the **Use the Office Assistant** checkbox.

5 Click **OK** to set the options selected or **Cancel** to leave things as they were.

The Office Assistant can remain visible as you work on a document, or you can hide it and call on it as required. If you leave it displayed, drag it to an area of your screen where it doesn't obscure your work.

♦ If you leave the Assistant displayed, click on it any time you want to ask a question.

♦ To hide the Office Assistant, right-click on it and choose **Hide** from the pop-up menu.

Tips

If you select any **Show Tips About** options on the **Options** tab in the **Customize** dialog box, the Office Assistant will constantly monitor your actions. If it thinks that it has a tip that may be useful to you, a light bulb will light up beside it. To read its tip, click the bulb.

ScreenTips

If you point to any tool on a toolbar, a ScreenTip will probably appear to describe the purpose of the tool. If no ScreenTips appear, you can easily switch them on if you want to.

If you like using keyboard shortcuts, you may find it useful to customize the basic ScreenTip, so that it displays the keyboard shortcut for a command as well. This might help you learn the keyboard shortcuts more quickly.

To customize ScreenTips:

1 Point to any toolbar and click the right mouse button.

2 Choose **Customize...** from the shortcut menu.

3 In the **Customize** dialog box select the **Options** tab.

4 To switch the ScreenTips on, select the **Show ScreenTips on toolbars** option (or deselect this to switch them off).

5 Select the **Show shortcut keys in ScreenTips** option to have the keyboard shortcut for each tool displayed in the ScreenTip.

6 Click **Close**.

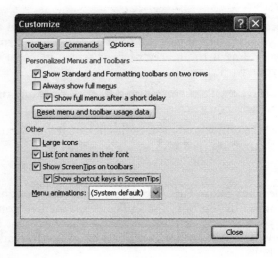

Dialog Box Help

When you access a dialog box in PowerPoint, for example, the **Customize** one, you can get Help on how to use it.

To get Help from within a dialog box:

1 Click the **Help** button 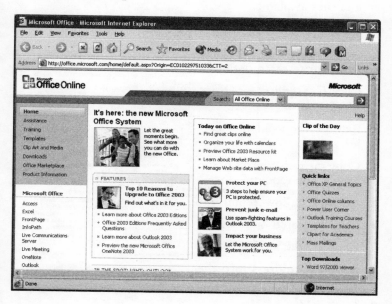 at the right of its title bar.

2 Explore the Help panel that is displayed.

1.9 Help on the Internet

If you can't find the Help you are looking for in the offline Help system, visit Microsoft Office Online to get updated Help files, answers to frequently-asked questions on PowerPoint, tips, templates and answers to top support issues.

1 Open the **Help** menu.

2 Choose **Microsoft Office Online**.

3 Navigate your way through the Help pages until you find the information required.

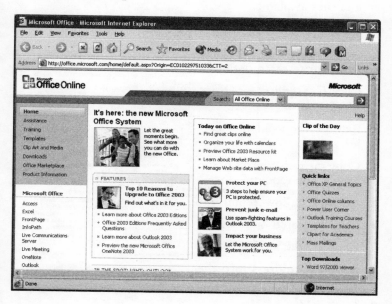

1.10 Research

The research feature enables you to find information on your computer or online without leaving PowerPoint. It includes a thesaurus, translation tools and online reference sites. It's easy to use and you can customize its settings to suit your needs. You can access Research from the Search Results Task Pane or from the Standard toolbar.

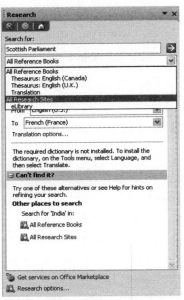

1 Click the **Research** tool on the Standard toolbar.

2 Type in the word/phrase you want to research.

3 Choose your research places from the reference books and sites available.

4 Click 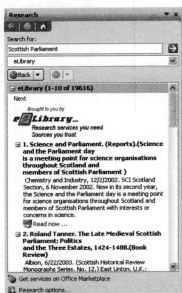.

You can easily add reference sites to your research options.

1 Click *Get services on Office Marketplace.*

2 Explore the available services.

3 Copy the web address of the service you require.

4 Go back to PowerPoint.

5 Click **Research options...**

6 Choose **Add Services...**

7 Paste the address into the Address box.

8 Click **Add**.

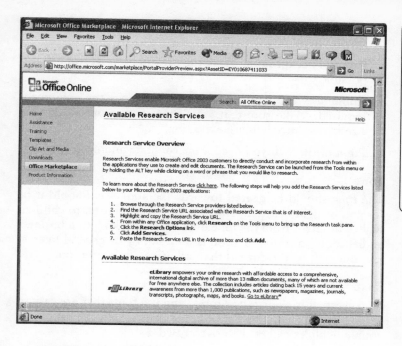

1.11 Design tips

For a presentation to be successful it's not just a case of using all the bells and whistles at your disposal. You must plan everything carefully to guarantee the success of your presentation.

Things that will influence your presentation include:

* **Audience size:** One-to-one, small group or a large gathering?

* **Knowledge:** Is your audience expert or novice? Will you need to go over the background to the presentation? Are elementary explanations required? Too much explanation to an audience that is familiar with the subject could cause it to lose interest. Too little to those new to the subject can have the same effect.

* **Age:** Are you presenting to children or adults?

* **Occupation:** Are you presenting to business people, students, retired?

- **Attention span:** Children normally have a shorter attention span than adults.
- **Cultural background:** Make the presentation relevant to it if possible.
- **Room size and lighting:** This will influence the equipment required. Make sure that your room is appropriate for the size of audience you are expecting.
- **Equipment:** Will you need a microphone and/or projector?

Tone

The *tone* should be geared towards the audience. Should it be formal, or light hearted? The tone of a presentation to children will be different from the tone used when speaking to a business audience. If your presentation is on a hobby or general interest the tone will be less formal than a business presentation.

Text

Be consistent in your use of fonts, and use fonts that are easy to read. If you have a long list of bullet points, split the list over a couple of slides rather than overcrowd a slide.

Lower case is generally easier to read than all capitals or initial capitals in bulleted lists. (It's also easier to type!)

Remember the 666 rule:

- no more that 6 consecutive slides should be text slides
- no more than 6 bullet points to a slide
- no more than 6 words to a bullet point.

Keep it short and simple!

Colour

Careful consideration needs to be given to *slide colour* and *text colour* so that the slides can be seen clearly by your audience. Don't use lots of different coloured backgrounds, and keep the contrast between the text and background colour high so that your audience can read the text easily. If possible, check that your choice of colours can be clearly read by the back row of your audience before you give your presentation.

You'll find some useful tips on colour at **office.microsoft.com/ assistance** – look for 'Choose the right colours for your PowerPoint presentation'.

Timing

How long will your presentation be? It may be up to you, in which case you should make sure that you give yourself enough time to get your points across, but don't ramble on unnecessarily (your audience will get bored).

You may have been given a specific amount of time, in which case you will need to time yourself as you practise your presentation. You might need to tailor the content of your presentation to fit into the time available.

Final checklist

You must give careful thought as to the best way to present your information – you want your audience to remember it!

Things to bear in mind include:

* Graphics – pictures, images and charts – often have more impact than words so use these where appropriate.

* Text is there to *support* the presentation.

* Don't overdo the detail in graphical and text information.

* Keep a consistent design scheme – it enhances clarity.

* Don't overdo the special effects – it confuses the audience and detracts from your message.

* Make sure that the presentation makes sense – check that your slides are in a logical order!

PowerPoint gives you the tools that you need to make effective presentations, but the way in which you use them will significantly affect the success (or otherwise) of your presentations.

1.12 Exiting PowerPoint

When you have finished working in PowerPoint you must close the application down – don't just switch off your computer.

♦ Open the **File** menu and choose **Exit**.

Or

♦ Click the **Close** button ☒ in the right-hand corner of the Application Title Bar.

If you have been working on a presentation but have not saved it you will be prompted to do so – see section 2.2.

Summary

In this chapter we have discussed:

♦ PowerPoint as a powerful presentation graphics package

♦ **The minimum software and hardware requirements necessary to run the package successfully**

♦ The installation procedure for the software

♦ PowerPoint objects

♦ Accessing the package through the Start menu

♦ The PowerPoint screen

♦ **Utilizing the menu system using the mouse and the keyboard**

♦ The Office Assistant and the Online Help system

♦ Research from within PowerPoint

♦ Design tips for presentations

♦ Exiting PowerPoint

02

basic powerpoint skills

In this chapter you will learn:

- how to create, save, print, open and close presentations
- about the view options
- about the outline and slides pane, and the notes pane
- how to hide and restore panes
- how to move through slides

Aims of this chapter

In this chapter we will discuss the options for creating a new presentation and saving, closing and opening existing presentations. We will also discuss the different view options that are available when working on a presentation.

2.1 New presentations

At startup

When you start PowerPoint, a new blank presentation is created automatically, with a blank title slide. The **Getting Started** Task Pane is displayed down the right of the screen.

The boxes with dotted outlines that appear when you create a new slide are called *placeholders*. Different slide layouts have different placeholders set up on them. They will contain the title, text and any other objects you display on your slide.

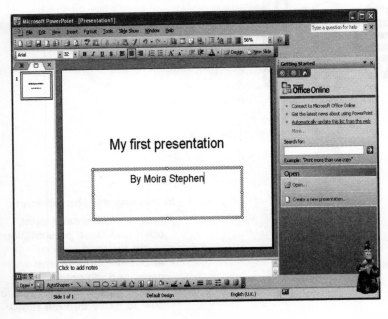

1 Follow the prompts on the slide – enter the title and subtitle (if required) for your presentation.

2 Click the **New Slide** tool 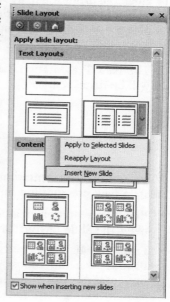 New Slide on the Formatting toolbar.

3 Select a layout from the Slide Layout Task Pane (a single bulleted list layout is the default).

4 Enter your text – follow the prompts.

5 Repeat steps 2 to 4 until all slides have been added.

♦ To insert a slide from the Slide Layout Task Pane click the drop-down arrow to the right of its icon, and click **Insert New Slide**.

♦ To resize the Task Pane click and drag its left border.

♦ Use the arrows at the top left to move between the Getting Started Task Pane and Slide Layout Task Pane.

Some of the slide layouts in the Slide Layout Task Pane have graphic, table, organization chart and clip art objects set up on them. We will look at these later in the book.

From within PowerPoint

To create a new presentation once PowerPoint is running:

♦ Click the **New tool** on the Standard toolbar. This creates a new presentation using the Default template. A blank title slide is displayed ready for you to complete.

Alternatively, you can use the New Presentation Task Pane.

To display the New Presentation Task Pane:

♦ Press [Ctrl]–[N].

Or

- Choose **New** from the **File** menu.

Or

1 Click the drop-down arrow to the right of the Task Pane title to display a list of the Task Panes.

2 Select **New Presentation**.

The New Presentation Task Pane will be displayed.

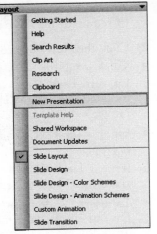

When the **New Presentation** Task Pane is displayed, you can create a new presentation in a number of ways.

- **Blank Presentation** creates a new blank presentation and displays the **Slide Layout** Task Pane (see above).

- **From Design Template** first displays the Slide Design Task Pane so you can choose a template on which to base your presentation (this will determine the design of the presentation, including font and colour scheme).

- **From AutoContent Wizard** creates a new presentation and starts a wizard to step you through the process of setting up your title slide, outline of presentation and colour scheme.

- **From Existing Presentation** creates a new presentation from one that you have saved.

Design Template

To create a new presentation using the Design Template:

1 Click **From Design Template** on the New Presentation Task Pane.

2 Select a template from those listed (or click **Browse...** and locate the template you wish to use).

3 Complete the Title Slide, replacing the prompts, e.g. *Click to add title*, with your own text.

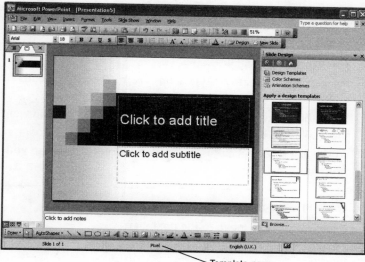

Template name

4 Click the ⊟ New Slide tool on the Formatting toolbar.

5 Select the layout for your next slide.

6 Follow the instructions on the slide to complete it.

7 Repeat steps 4 to 6 until all slides have been added.

If you don't like the look of your selected template, change it from the **Slide Design** Task Pane.

To display the Slide Design Task Pane:

◆ Click the **Design** tool ✏ Design on the Formatting toolbar.

Or

◆ Click the drop-down arrow at the top right of the Task Pane and choose **Slide Design** from the list.

Or

◆ Double-click on the template name on the Status Bar.

AutoContent Wizard

This sets up several slides – the exact number depends on the choices you make as you work through the Wizard. If you need help setting up the structure of your presentation, or need some ideas on what to put on your slides, this option may be useful.

1 Click **From AutoContent Wizard** on the Task Pane and click [Next >] at the first step.

2 Pick the option that best describes the type of presentation you are going to give.

3 Select the presentation style – on-screen, Web, overheads or slides.

4 Enter the presentation title and any information that you want displayed in the slide footer area.

5 At the last screen click [Finish]. PowerPoint will set up your presentation.

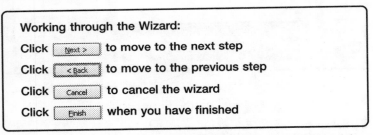

Working through the Wizard:

Click [Next >] to move to the next step

Click [< Back] to move to the previous step

Click [Cancel] to cancel the wizard

Click [Finish] when you have finished

• Once a presentation has been created, you can add or delete slides, change slide layouts or the design template as required.

2.2 Saving a presentation

Once you have set up your presentation, you must save it if you want to keep it (if you don't save it, it will be lost when you close PowerPoint or switch off your computer).

1 Click the **Save** tool ▣ on the Standard toolbar.

2 Specify the drive and/or folder into which you wish to save your presentation.

3 Give your presentation a file name.

4 Click **Save**.

Save vs Save As

The first time you save a presentation, you are taken to the **Save As** dialog box where you specify the drive and/or folder that you want your file saved in, and give your presentation a name. There-

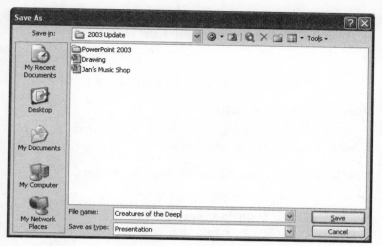

after, any time you save the presentation using the **Save** tool 🖫 on the toolbar, the old version of the file is replaced by the new, edited version. This is what you would usually want to happen.

However, if you have saved your presentation, gone on to edit it, then wish to save the edited version using a different file name, or in a different location, open the **File** menu and choose **Save As** to get to the **Save As** dialog box.

2.3 Closing and opening files

When you've finished working on your presentation you must save it (see above) and close it.

Leaving PowerPoint is very easy. If you use other Windows packages, the technique is very similar.

Closing a presentation

♦ Open the **File** menu and choose **Close**.

Or

♦ Click **Close window** 🗙 on the Presentation title bar.

♦ If you have made changes to your presentation since you last saved it, you will be prompted to save them before the file is closed. If you want to save, choose **Yes** at the prompt.

Leaving PowerPoint

♦ Open the **File** menu and choose **Exit**.

Or

♦ Click the **Close** ▨ button on the PowerPoint title bar.

Opening a presentation

If you want to work on a presentation you've already created, saved and closed, you must open it first.

1 Click the **Open** tool ▨ on the Standard toolbar.

Or

♦ Open the **File** menu and choose **Open**.

2 Select the drive and folder that contains your presentation file.

3 Double-click on the name or select it and click ▨ Open ▾

♦ Recently used files are displayed at the end of the **File** menu – to open one simply click on its name.

2.4 View options

When working on a presentation, there are three view options:

♦ Normal view

♦ Slide Sorter view

♦ Slide Show

By default, PowerPoint opens a presentation in **Normal** view.

Use the View icons ▨▨▨ at the bottom left of the screen to get a different view of your presentation. You can also change views using the **View** menu.

The **View** menu has an additional option called **Notes Page** view. This displays a miniature of your slide, with the notes area below it, which is how your notes will look when printed. You can enter and edit your notes in this view. If you wish to do this, use the **Zoom** tool on the Standard toolbar to zoom in to about 75% so that you can read the text.

In **Slide Sorter** view each slide is displayed in miniature – this view can be used for moving slides around and to help you prepare for the actual presentation. We will discuss this view later in the book.

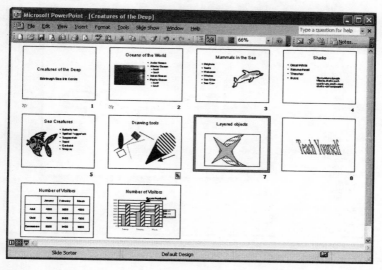

Slide Show view can be useful at any time to let you see how your slide will look in the final presentation. Press **[Esc]** from Slide Show view to return to your presentation file.

The view that you will use when setting up your presentation is **Normal** view. In Normal view, you have three panes displaying different parts of your presentation: the slide itself, a notes pane displayed at the bottom and the outline and slide tabs displayed down the left.

A Task Pane will often be displayed too.

2.5 Outline and Slides pane

In Normal view the Outline and Slides pane is displayed down the left of the screen.

The Outline tab displays the text on each slide, with a slide icon to the left of each slide title.

Outline tab   Slides tab

Slide icon

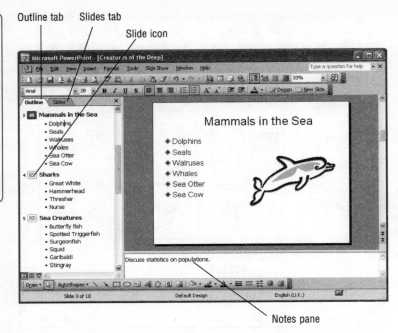

Notes pane

You can insert and delete text in the Outline tab just as you would on the Slide itself.

You can select a slide on the Outline tab by clicking the slide icon to the left of the title.

The Slides tab shows miniatures of the slides in the presentation.

2.6 Notes pane

As the presenter, you may wish to add some notes (that you can use during your presentation) to some of your slides.

Notes are added to the Notes pane, below the Slide pane.

To add notes:

1   Click in the **Notes** pane.

2   Type in your notes.

We will discuss notes more fully in Chapter 9.

2.7 Hide/Restore panes

To hide panes:

♦ Click **Close** ▓ at the top right of the Outline and Slides pane. Both this and the Notes pane will disappear.

To restore panes:

♦ Click the **Normal view** icon or open the **View** menu and choose **Normal (Restore Panes)**.

To resize the Outline and Slides pane:

♦ Click and drag on its right border.

To resize the Notes Slides pane:

♦ Click and drag its top border.

2.8 Moving through the slides

To move through the slides in your presentation:

♦ Click on the slide that you wish to display on the Slides tab.

Or

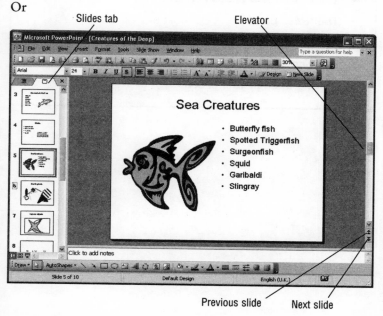

Slides tab   Elevator

Previous slide   Next slide

- Click the **Next** or **Previous Slide** buttons at the bottom of the vertical scroll bar.

Or

- Drag the elevator on the vertical scroll bar up and down (let go when you reach the required slide).

Summary

This chapter has introduced what you need to know to get started using PowerPoint. We have discussed:

- Creating a new presentation using the Blank Presentation, Design Template and AutoContent Wizard

- Adding slides to a presentation

- Saving a presentation, including Save vs Save As

- Closing and opening a presentation

- The view options available in a presentation

- The Outline and Slides pane

- The Notes pane

- Hiding and Restoring the panes

- Resizing the panes

- Moving through your slides

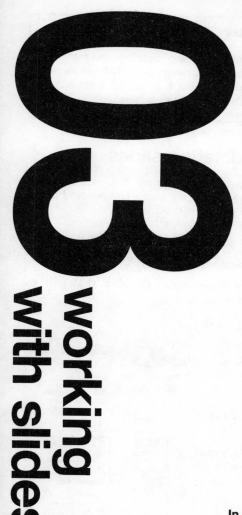

03 working with slides

In this chapter you will learn:

- how to add, delete, move and copy slides
- how to format text
- about indents, numbering and bullet points
- how to change the slide layout and the template
- how to add comments

Aims of this chapter

In this chapter we will discuss adding, deleting and moving slides. We will also discuss structuring the bullet points on a slide, rearranging the order of the bullets and numbering the points on a slide (rather than using bullets).

3.1 Adding and deleting slides

We discussed adding slides in Normal view in Chapter 2, but you can also add slides in Slide Sorter view. The method is the same in either view.

Adding a slide

If the Slide Layout Task Pane is not displayed:

1 View (or select in Slide Sorter view) the slide that will go *before* the slide you are going to add.

2 Click the `New Slide` tool on the Formatting toolbar.

3 Choose a slide layout from the Slide Layout Task Pane.

If the Slide Layout Task Pane is open:

1 View (or select in Slide Sorter view) the slide that will go *before* the slide you are going to add.

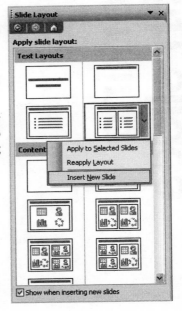

2 Click the drop-down arrow to the right of the slide layout that you wish to insert.

3 Click **Insert New Slide**.

Deleting a slide

In Normal view:

1 View the slide that you wish to delete.

2 Open the **Edit** menu and click **Delete Slide**.

In the Outline and Slides pane or in Slide Sorter view:

1 Select the slide that you wish to delete.

2 Press [Delete].

3.2 Moving or copying a slide

This can be done in the Outline and Slides pane or in Slide Sorter view.

Drag and drop

1 Select the slide that you wish to move.

2 To move the slide – drag and drop it (watching the dimmed line to check your position).

Or

◆ To copy the slide – hold down [Ctrl] while you drag and drop it into place.

Cut or copy and paste

1 Select the slide that you wish to move.

2 Click the **Cut** tool ✄ (or the **Copy** ▦ tool) on the Standard toolbar.

3 Select the slide that you want to precede the slide you are moving or copying.

4 Click the **Paste** tool ▦ on the Standard toolbar.

Cut or Copy

When you drag and drop or cut and paste a slide, the slide is actually *moved* from one place to another.

If you [Ctrl]-drag and drop or copy and paste a slide, the original slide remains where it is, and a copy is created where you drop or paste the slide.

3.3 Formatting text

So far, we've accepted the font formats set by PowerPoint. You can change these at any time using the Formatting toolbar.

To change the font:

1 Select the text you want to format.

2 Drop down the **Font** list and choose one.

3 Deselect the text.

To change the font colour:

1 Select the text.

2 Drop down the colour palette by clicking the drop-down arrow to the right of the **Font Color** tool, and choose one.

To change the font size:

1 Select the text.

2 Drop down the **Font size** list and choose one.

Or

• Click 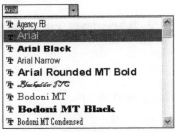 to increase or 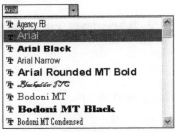 to decrease it to the next size in the Font Size list.

To change the font style:

1 Select the text.

2 Click the **Bold** 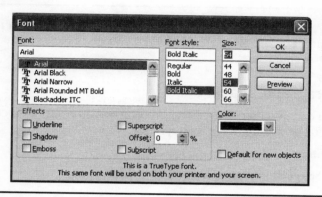, **Italic**, **Underline** or **Shadow** tools to switch the format on and off.

You can also go to the **Font** dialog box to format the text on your slides.

1 Select the text to be formatted.

2 Choose **Font...** from the **Format** menu.

3 Set the formatting options as required.

4 Click **OK**.

Useful keyboard shortcuts

[Ctrl]-[B] Bold   [Ctrl]-[I] Italics
[Ctrl]-[U] Underline

These all toggle the effect on and off

3.4 Paragraph formatting

Alignment

In presentations, text is usually aligned left or centred. There are tools for both of these, and for right alignment, on the Formatting toolbar. If you want text justified (making the text meet both left and right margins), open the **Format** menu, point to **Alignment** and select **Justify**.

1 Select the text you want to format.

2 Click the **Left** 🔲, **Center** 🔲 or **Right** 🔲 **Alignment** tool.

3 If you have selected multiple paragraphs or several characters, deselect the text.

Useful keyboard shortcuts

[Ctrl]-[L] Left Align   [Ctrl]-[R] Right Align
[Ctrl]-[E] Center   [Ctrl]-[J] Justify

◆ A paragraph is selected if the insertion point is within it, or at least part of it is highlighted – you don't need to select all the characters.

Paragraph spacing

You can distribute the bullet points on a slide evenly by increasing or decreasing the paragraph spacing as necessary.

To increase the paragraph spacing:

1 Select the paragraphs.

2 Click the **Increase Paragraph Spacing** tool 🔲.

To decrease the paragraph spacing:

1 Select the paragraphs.

2 Click the **Decrease Paragraph Spacing** tool 🔲.

The paragraph spacing is increased or decreased by 0.1 each time you click the Increase or Decrease Paragraph Spacing tool.

Line spacing

The line spacing of bullet points is normally set to single, with 0.2 spacing before each paragraph, and 0 spacing after the paragraph.

These options can be changed in the Line Spacing dialog box.

To change the line spacing:

1 Open the **Format** menu.

2 Choose **Line Spacing...**

3 Set the spacing options in the **Line Spacing** dialog box.

4 Click **Preview** if you want to view the effect of your selections.

5 Click **OK** to apply the options (or **Cancel** if you want to leave things as they were).

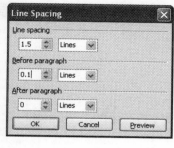

AutoFit

If you type in more text than will fit into a Title or Body text placeholder, PowerPoint will 'AutoFit' the text into it.

An AutoFit button will appear, with a drop-down set of options.

1 Click the arrow to see the options.

2 Select an option.

Auto Formatting options are specified in the AutoCorrect dialog box.

To display this dialog box:

1 Click **Control AutoCorrect Options...** at the bottom of the **AutoFit Options** list.

Or

From the **Tools** menu choose **AutoCorrect Options...**

2 Select the **AutoFormat As You Type** tab.

3 Specify the options required.

4 Click **OK**.

An option button is also displayed when you type in an Internet or network path. The text is automatically converted to a hyperlink, and a button allows you to control the activity if you wish.

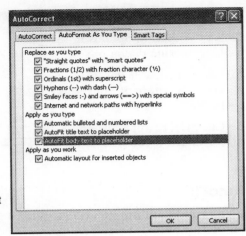

Explore the options in the
AutoCorrect and AutoFormat
As You Type tabs in the
AutoCorrect dialog box.

3.5 Bullet points

The text on your slide can be structured into main points and subpoints if necessary (using up to 5 levels).

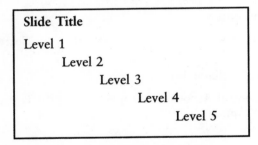

The default level for a bullet point is Level 1.

You can easily increase the indent of bullet points so that you create subpoints under your main points if required. You can decrease the indent again if you change your mind.

To increase or decrease the indent on a bullet point:

Using the toolbar

1 Click anywhere within the bullet point you wish to demote (either on your slide or on the **Outline** tab).

Oceans of the World

- **Arctic Ocean**
- **Atlantic Ocean**
  - North
  - South
- **Indian Ocean**
- **Pacific Ocean**
  - North
  - South

---

2 Click **Increase Indent** [⬛] on the Formatting toolbar to demote or **Decrease Indent** [⬛] to promote the bullet.

Drag

You can also drag the bullet points to the level required.

1 Move the mouse pointer over the bullet (it becomes a four-headed arrow when it is in the correct position).

2 Drag the bullet right or left to the required level (the pointer will become a two-headed arrow as you drag).

Using the keyboard

1 Place the insertion point before the text that you wish to increase or decrease the indent of.

2 Press [**Tab**] to increase the indent.

Or

♦ Press [**Shift**]-[**Tab**] to decrease the indent.

Rearranging the points

If you have entered your text, and then decide that it is not in the correct order, you can move the points within (or between) slides.

To move the points within a slide:

Cut or copy and paste

1 Select the bullet point that you wish to move.

2 Click the **Cut** tool  (or the **Copy** tool) on the Standard toolbar.

3 Place the insertion point at the beginning of the text in the bullet point that will go below the point that you are moving or copying.

4 Click the **Paste** tool on the Standard toolbar.

- Depending on the object pasted, the Paste Options button appears. The options available give you greater control over the formatting of the pasted item.

  Keep Source Formatting

  Use Design Template Formatting

Drag

You can also drag the bullet points to the position required.

1 Move the pointer over the bullet to get the four-headed arrow.

2 Drag the bullet up or down to the required position.

Using the keyboard

1 Place the insertion point within the text that you wish to move up or down.

2 Press [**Alt**]-[**Shift**]-[**Up arrow**] to move the point up.

Or

- Press [**Alt**]-[**Shift**]-[**Down arrow**] to move the point down.

Numbering the points

There may be times that you would rather number your points than use bullets. You can use the Numbering tool on the Formatting toolbar for this.

1 Select the points that you want numbered.

2 Click the **Numbering** tool .

Numbered points can be promoted, demoted and moved in the same way as bulleted points.

Removing bullets or numbers

You will nearly always want the points on your slide to be bulleted or numbered for easy identification. There may, however, be odd occasions when you wish to switch the bullets or numbers off altogether.

To switch the bullets or numbers off:

1 Select the points on your slide.

2 If the points are bulleted, click the **Bullets** tool ▦ to switch them off.

Or

♦ If the points are numbered, click the **Numbering** tool ▦ to switch them off.

Customized bullets

The bullet style will normally be picked up from the Design Template used for the presentation. As an alternative, you could select a bullet from the Bullets and Numbering dialog box.

1 Select the point(s).

2 Open the **Format** menu and choose **Bullets and Numbering**.

3 Click on the **Bulleted** tab.

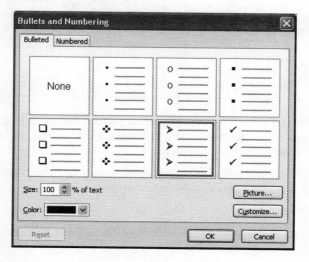

4 Select a bullet.

5 Set the size and colour as required.

6 Click **OK**.

You could also choose a different character from one of the fonts available for your bullet point.

1 Work through steps 1 to 3 above.

2 Click **Customize...**

3 In the **Symbol** dialog box, select a font from the list and choose a character – click on it.

Or

◆ Select a character from the **Recently used symbols:** row.

4 Click **OK** to close the **Symbol** dialog box.

5 Click **OK** to close the **Bullets and Numbering** dialog box.

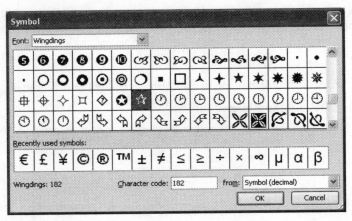

◆ Alternatively, you can choose a picture bullet if you click **Picture...** in the **Bullets and Numbering** dialog box, and select a bullet from those available.

◆ You can customize the numbering style from the **Numbered** tab in the **Bullets and Numbering** dialog box.

3.6 Slide layout

Each time you add a new slide you choose the layout for it. You can easily change the layout of any existing slide if you decide that another would be more suitable.

To change the slide layout:

1 View the slide in **Normal View**.

2 Display the Slide Layout Task Pane.

♦ Choose **Slide Layout** from the Task Pane list.

Or

♦ Click the [Layout] tool on the Formatting toolbar.

Or

♦ Choose **Slide Layout...** from the Format menu.

3 Select the layout required.

3.7 Design template

Each presentation uses a design template. This is a file that contains information on the type and size of bullets and fonts to be used, placeholder sizes and positions, background design and fill colour schemes, and a slide master and optional title master.

If you create a presentation using the *Blank Presentation* option, the default design template is used. If you create a presentation using the *From Design Template*, or *From AutoContent Wizard* options, a professionally designed template is used.

You can apply a different design template to your file at any time.

To change the design template:

1 Display the Slide Design Task Pane.

♦ Choose **Slide Design** from the Task Pane list.

Or

♦ Click the [Design] tool on the Formatting toolbar.

Or

♦ Choose **Slide Design...** from the **Format** menu.

Or

♦ Double-click the current design name on the Status Bar.

2 Select the design required.

You can create your own design templates. You should also read Chapter 8 on Masters if you want to do this.

If a presentation is in sections, you could apply a different de-sign template to the different parts of it. You can select multiple slides in the Slide Pane on the left, or in Slide Sorter view, and apply a design template to the selected slides.

To create your own design template:

1 Create a new presentation – either from scratch or from an existing presentation. If you are using an ex-isting one that you want to keep, select *From existing presentation* in the New Presentation Task Pane, and click **Create New** to preserve your original presentation.

2 Edit the file – delete any text, slides, or design elements that you don't want to be part of the new template, and apply any changes that you do want in the template.

3 Click [icon] to display the **Save As** dialog box.

4 Enter a name for your template in the **File Name** field.

5 Choose *Design Template* in the **Save as type** field.

6 Click **Save.**

7 Close the template.

The template will be listed in the Slide Design Task Pane, under *Available for Use* the next time you open PowerPoint or in the *Recently Used Templates* list in the New Presentation Task Pane.

3.8 Comments

If you are working on a presentation and wish to add a comment to a slide, perhaps a reminder to yourself to check something, you can use Comments. These will not be displayed when you give your presentation. You have the option of printing any comments when you print your presentation (see Chapter 11).

To add a comment to a slide:

1 Display the slide in Normal view.

2 Open the **Insert** menu.

3 Choose **Comment**.

4 Type in your comment.

5 Click anywhere on your slide when you have finished.

A comment marker is displayed on the slide in Normal view. If you move the pointer over it, the comment will be displayed.

To edit a comment:

1 Right-click on it.

2 Left-click on **Edit Comment**.

3 Update the comment as necessary.

4 Press [Esc] or click anywhere on your slide when you have finished.

To delete a comment:

1 Right-click on it.

2 Left-click on **Delete Comment**.

To copy the comment text:

1 Right-click on the comment.

2 Left-click on **Copy Text**.

3 Paste the text where required.

When you insert a comment the Reviewing toolbar is displayed. You can use this toolbar to work with your comments.

The Reviewing toolbar

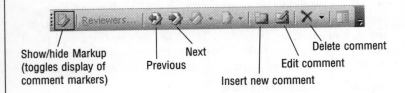

Show/hide Markup
(toggles display of
comment markers)

Previous

Next

Insert new comment

Edit comment

Delete comment

+ See Chapter 14 for more on switching toolbars on and off.

3.9 Headers and footers

You can control the date options, switch on slide numbering, or enter text for the footer area in the Header and Footer dialog box. You can access this dialog box in Normal view or in Master view.

1 Open the **View** menu and choose **Header and Footer**.

2 Select the **Slide** tab.

3 Complete the dialog box as required.

4 Click **Apply to All** or **Apply**.

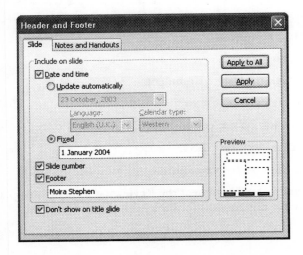

Summary

This chapter has discussed:

- Adding slides
- Deleting slides
- Moving and copying slides
- Formatting text
- Increasing and decreasing the indent on bullet points
- Moving bullet points
- Numbering points
- Removing bullets and numbers from points
- Customizing bullet points
- Changing the slide layout
- Design templates
- Adding, editing, deleting and copying comments
- Defining headers and footers

04

drawing

In this chapter you will learn:

- about drawing objects
- how to add special effects to drawing objects
- what AutoShapes are
- how to change the order, and group and ungroup objects
- how to create WordArt objects

Aims of this chapter

So far, we have dealt with text objects – slide headings and points listed for discussion on the slides. In this chapter we will consider some of the other objects that you may want to place on your slide. Moving, resizing and deleting objects, drawings tools, AutoShapes, rotating and grouping objects, and WordArt will be discussed.

4.1 Basic object handling skills

The objects on a slide can be manipulated in a variety of ways. Once an object has been selected, you can move it, resize it, delete it (and lots of other things as we'll soon see).

Work in Normal view for this section.

To select a text object:

1 Position the mouse pointer over any text within the placeholder area and click.

♦ Note the handles that appear at the corners and along the edges of the selected object.

To select other objects:

♦ Click anywhere inside the object placeholder.

To deselect an object:

♦ Click anywhere outside the selected object.

To move an object:

♦ Point to the border of a text object, or anywhere within any other type of object (not a handle) and drag the object to its new position.

To resize an object:

♦ Point to one of the handles (note the mouse pointer) and drag the handle until the object is the required size.

To delete a text object:

♦ Select the text object, click the border once, then press [Delete].

To delete other objects:

♦ Select, and then press [**Delete**].

To undo a mistake:

♦ If you delete an object by mistake, click 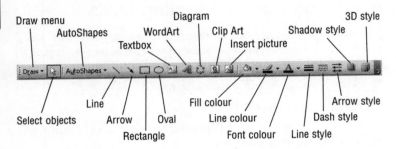 the **Undo** tool on the Standard toolbar.

The Drawing toolbar

The Drawing toolbar is normally displayed along the bottom of the window.

4.2 Text box tool

You can use the Text box tool to enter text anywhere on your slide (not necessarily within an existing text placeholder).

1 Select the **Text Box** tool ▣.

2 Click anywhere on your slide to position the insertion point.

3 Key in the text.

4 Format the text as required.

The text object you have created can be selected, moved, resized and deleted. You can format the text using any of the formatting options – bold, size, font style, italics, underline, etc.

Text objects can be placed in an AutoShape to add emphasis, or rotated to create interesting effects on your slides (see section 4.4).

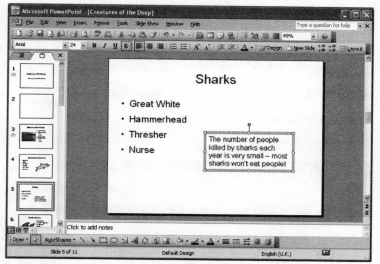

Text boxes allow you to add text anywhere on a slide.

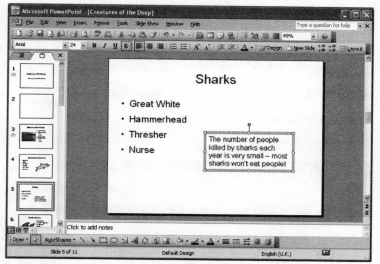

4.3 Drawing tools

The line, arrow, rectangle and oval tools all work in a similar way. You can customize a shape in many ways – give it a shadow or 3D effect, change the line colour and thickness, or experiment with fill colours and patterns.

Experiment with the options on your slides.

To use the line-based tools:

1 Select a tool – line, arrow, rectangle or oval [\\ □ ○].

2 Click and drag to draw the shape.

◆ Hold [Shift] down as you click and drag if you want a straight line (Line tool), a square (Rectangle tool) or circle (Oval tool).

Different effects

You can format the drawing objects by changing the fill colour or line colour, changing the line or arrow style, or giving the object a shadow or 3D effect.

To format the object:

1 Select the object – click anywhere within it.

+ Change the Fill or Line colour [icon].

+ Set the line, dash or arrow style [icon].

+ Add a shadow or 3D effect [icon].

2 Deselect the object.

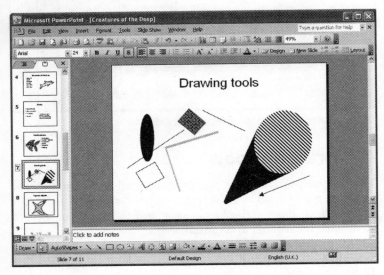

+ If you need to draw several lines, arrows, rectangles or ovals, you can 'lock' the tool on by double-clicking on it. Draw as many shapes as you need, then select any other tool (or press **[Esc]**) to unlock it.

4.4 AutoShapes

You may find the shape you need under AutoShapes. If you want stars, triangles, arrows, etc. on your slide you'll find lots to choose from. AutoShapes can be drawn and formatted in the same way as the basic drawing shapes.

Experiment with the options.

To create an autoshape:

1 Click the **AutoShapes** tool to display the categories available.

2 Select a category.

3 Choose a shape.

4 Click and drag on your slide to draw your shape.

5 Drag a corner or side handle to change the size.

6 Drag the diamond-shaped handle to adjust the shape.

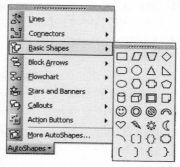

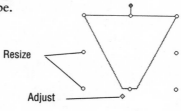

Resize

Adjust

The Freeform and Curve AutoShapes in the Line category don't quite follow the basic click and drag principle adopted by the other drawing tools.

To draw a freeform line:

♦ Click and drag (note the pencil shaped pointer) to draw lines freehand.

Or

♦ Click where you want the line to start, then click again where it will end, to get a straight line.

To draw a curve:

♦ Click a path that you want the curve to follow.

To stop drawing:

♦ Double-click or press [Esc] when done to switch the tool off.

You can change the fill colour or pattern or line characteristics of any shape using the tools on the Drawing toolbar.

More AutoShapes

1 Select **More AutoShapes...** from the AutoShapes list.

2 Scroll through the list of AutoShapes displayed.

3 Click on the shape that you want to insert.

◆ Move and/or resize the shape as required.

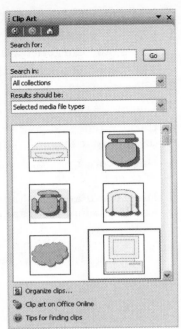

4.5 Rotate and Flip

Once an object has been drawn, you can flip it over horizontally or vertically, or rotate it right or left to get the effect you want.

1 Select the object you wish to rotate. Rotate handle

2 Drag the rotate handle to rotate the object.

Or

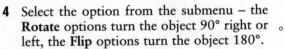

3 Choose **Rotate** or **Flip** from the **Draw** menu.

4 Select the option from the submenu – the **Rotate** options turn the object 90° right or left, the **Flip** options turn the object 180°.

◆ With the **Free Rotate** option, rotate handles appear on each corner of the object. Drag a rotate handle to turn the shape.

The **Rotate or Flip** submenu can be dragged to float on your screen. Click and drag its title bar. Any submenu with a title bar can become a floating menu.

4.6 Changing the order

When you draw objects onto your slides, they lie in layers in the order in which they are drawn. The first object is on the bottom layer, the next on a layer above the first one and so on. Using this, you can create complex drawings by overlapping objects.

If you need to rearrange the layering of your objects, you can do so using the Bring Forward and Send Backward commands.

1 Select the object to **Bring Forward** or **Send Backward**.
2 Open the **Draw** menu.
3 Select **Order**.
4 Choose the option required.

♦ **Bring to Front** and **Send to Back** move the selected object to the top or bottom of the pile of objects. **Bring Forward** and **Send Backward** move the selected object through the pile one layer at a time.

♦ Right-click on the selected object to open the shortcut menu. Select **Order** from it and specify the options required.

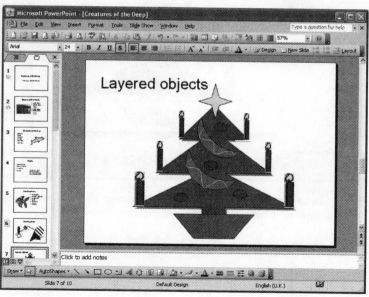

4.7 Group and Ungroup

If you have drawn several objects to generate an image, you can group the objects together into one to make it easier to move, copy or resize.

1 Select the objects you want to group.

◆ Select the first object then hold [**Shift**] down while you select the other objects.

◆ To select all the objects, use [**Ctrl**]-[**A**] or drag over them.

2 Open the **Draw** menu.

3 Select **Group**.

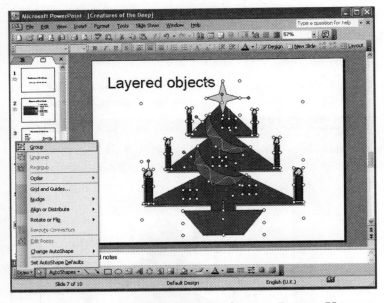

◆ To edit a grouped object, select it then use **Draw > Ungroup** to separate it into its original objects.

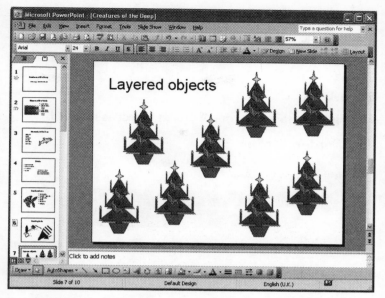

Grouped object resized and copied

4.8 WordArt

WordArt lets you create special text effects. You can produce stunning title slides and real eyecatchers wherever they are needed.

1 Click the **Insert WordArt** tool

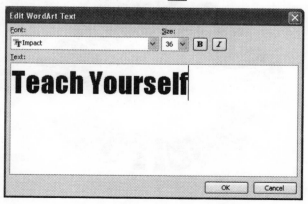

2 Select a WordArt style from the Gallery.

3 Click **OK**.

4 At the **Edit WordArt Text** dialog box, enter (and format) the text.

5 Click **OK**.

6 Adjust the shape of your WordArt object as required.

The WordArt toolbar

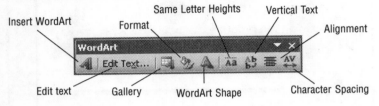

Insert WordArt · Format · Same Letter Heights · Vertical Text · Alignment · Edit text · Gallery · WordArt Shape · Character Spacing

◆ Experiment with the tools to see the effects they produce.

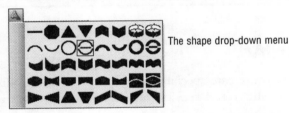

The shape drop-down menu

Summary

This chapter has introduced:

*   Selecting, moving, resizing and deleting objects
*   The drawing tools
*   Formatting drawing objects
*   AutoShapes
*   Rotating and grouping objects
*   Changing the order and layers of objects
*   WordArt

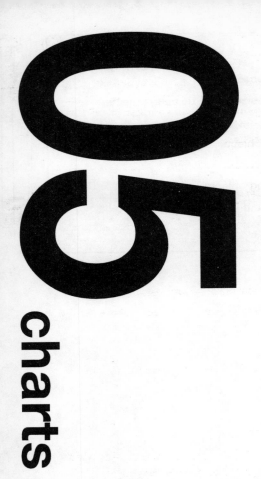

05

charts

In this chapter you will learn:

- how to create charts
- some chart formatting options
- about chart objects
- how to import a chart from Excel

Aims of this chapter

Pictures can speak louder than words – and when this is the case you can use graphs, organization charts, clip art, tables, etc. to help you make your point. In this chapter we'll look at ways you can add a chart or graph to a slide. We will create charts, work with datasheets, change the chart type, and customize the chart in a variety of ways.

5.1 Creating a chart

You can create charts from scratch within PowerPoint or import them from Microsoft Excel. The default charting program used by PowerPoint is Microsoft Graph, which is installed automatically with PowerPoint.

There are three main ways to set up your chart.

* Choose a slide with a **Chart** placeholder from the **Slide Layout** Task Pane.

Or

* Choose a new layout with a **Content** placeholder.

Or

* Click the **Insert Chart** tool.

To use a Chart placeholder:

* Double-click within the **Chart** placeholder to add a chart.

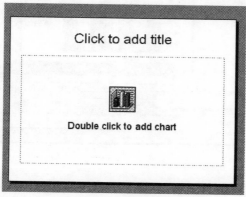

To use a Content placeholder:

Insert Chart

*   Click the **Insert Chart** tool in the placeholder.

To use a slide with no placeholder set:

*   Click the **Insert Chart** tool 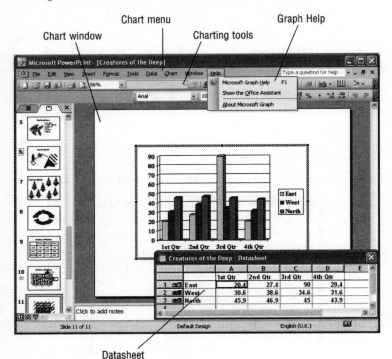 on the Standard toolbar.

Regardless of how you decide to create your chart, Microsoft Graph opens and a chart window is displayed. This has its own Standard and Formatting toolbars, and you will notice a **Chart** menu appear on the Menu bar. The options in the other menus change to those suitable for working on charts.

There is also a small Datasheet window (which can be moved or resized as necessary), where you can key in the data that you want to chart. When working in Microsoft Graph the Help menu will give you access to help pages on the program.

*   Explore the menus to see how they have changed.

Chart menu

Chart window

Charting tools

Graph Help

Datasheet

5.2 The datasheet

You must replace the sample data in the datasheet with the data you want to chart.

1 Select the cell into which you wish to enter your own data.

2 Key in the data.

3 Move to the next cell you want to work on – use any of the methods suggested below.

If you do not need to replace all the sample data, delete the rows or columns that are not required – select them and press the [Delete] key.

♦ To select a row, click the number on its left.

♦ To select a column, click the letter at the top.

You can adjust the width of a column by dragging the vertical line to the right of the column header.

Moving around the datasheet

There are a number of ways to move from cell to cell.

You can use the keys:

Arrow keys	one cell in direction of arrow
[Tab]	forward to the next cell
[Shift]-[Tab]	back to the previous cell
[Enter]	down to the next cell in a column

Or point to the cell and click.

The cell you are in (your *current* cell) has a dark border.

Standard toolbar

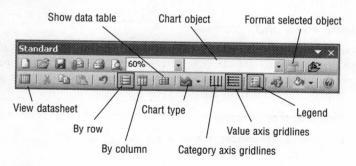

By Row or By Column

The Category axis has labels taken from the column or row headings. Use By Row and By Column on the Standard toolbar to indicate whether the data series is in rows or columns. A graphic in the row or column heading indicates the selected option.

Data series by row

Drag to adjust column width

Click to select column

Click to select row

Creatures of the Deep - Datasheet						
		A	B	C	D	E
		January	February	March	4th Qtr	
1	Adult	4000	5000	4000	20.4	
2	Child	7500	8400	7500	31.6	
3	Concessio	3500	5400	5500	43.9	
4						

If the data is plotted By Row, the row labels are displayed in the legend; when plotted By Column, the column headings are displayed in the legend.

* Don't enter too much data – the chart will be seen on a slide or overhead. If it's too detailed your audience may not fully appreciate it.

View/hide datasheet

Once you have keyed in your data, you can hide the datasheet so that you can see the chart clearly on your screen. If you hide your datasheet, you can easily view it again if you need to edit any data. Click the View Datasheet tool 📊 to view or hide it, as required.

Hiding rows and columns

You may have entered data into your datasheet, then decide that you don't wish to display it on the chart. If you don't want to actually delete the data, you can hide it. You can then unhide it to display it, rather than have to type it in again.

To hide a row or column:

1 Display the datasheet if necessary.

2 Double-click on the column heading – the letter at the top of the column – you wish to hide.

Or

3 Double-click the number to the left of the row.

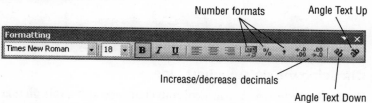

The data is dimmed and will not appear on the chart. To reveal the data again double-click on the column heading or row number.

Number formats

Numbers can be displayed in Currency, Percent or Comma styles.

Currency: £1,565.75   Percent: 156575%
Comma: 1,565.75

Select the cell(s), and click a style tool on the formatting toolbar.

Formatting toolbar

Number formats   Angle Text Up

Increase/decrease decimals

Angle Text Down

5.3 Chart Type

A column chart is the default – the type used unless you specify a different one. You can try out a variety of other chart types using the Chart Type tool on the Standard toolbar.

1 Click the drop-down arrow to display the chart types available.

2 Choose one.

Each chart type has a variety of subtypes. To access all the types and subtypes you must open the Chart Type dialog box.

1 Open the **Chart** menu.

2 Choose **Chart Type...**

3 Select the **Standard Types** tab.

4 Explore the options available.

5 Hold down the **Press and Hold to View Sample** button to display a preview of your chart.

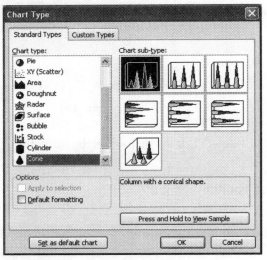

Changing the default chart type

If you do not normally use a column chart you can easily change the default chart type to the one that you use most often.

1 Select the chart type from the **Chart Type** dialog box.

2 Click the **Set as default chart** button.

3 Respond to the prompt asking if you are sure that you want to change the default chart type – click **Yes** if you are, **No** if you've changed your mind.

- You'll find even more chart types to choose from on the **Custom Types** tab.

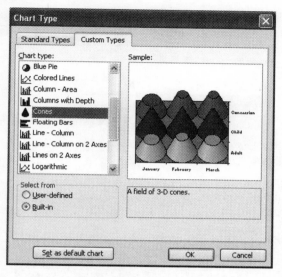

Adding your own custom chart type

If you have created a custom chart, e.g. a combination chart (see section 5.6) or one with overlapping data series (see section 5.7), and wish to reuse it, you can save it as a custom chart type.

1 Display the **Chart Type** dialog box.
2 Select the **Custom Types** tab.
3 Choose **User-Defined** in the **Select From** options.
4 Click **Add...**

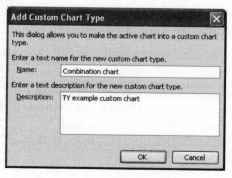

5 Give your chart a name (maximum 31 characters) and description (if you wish).

6 Click **OK**.

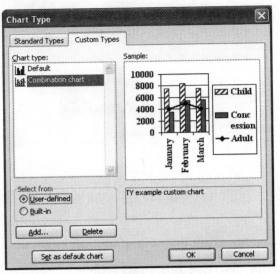

• Combination charts are discussed later in the chapter.

5.4 Chart objects

Each part of your chart is an object. The chart objects are:

• Category Axis   • Chart Area

• Corners   • Floor

• Legend   • Plot Area

• Series Axis   • Value Axis

• Walls   • Series

• Value Axis Major Gridlines

You can check where these objects are on your chart by using the Chart Objects tool. Select the object from the drop-down list, and look at your chart to see what has been selected – take a tour of the objects!

Formatting chart objects

You can format each object on your chart in a variety of ways. The formatting options vary from object to object.

To format an object:

1 Select it – click on it, or select it from the **Chart Object** list.

2 Click the **Format** tool 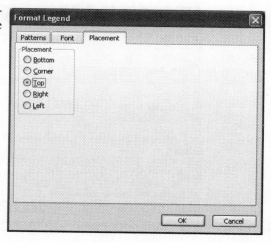 on the Standard toolbar.

Or

♦ Double-click on the object that you wish to format.

The Format dialog box for the object will be displayed. Explore the dialog box and experiment with its formatting options.

♦ The tools on the Formatting and Drawing toolbars can also be used to set the font size, colour, alignment, etc. of an object.

Try out the formatting suggested below to help get you started – then it's over to you to experiment!

Formatting the legend

The Format Legend dialog box contains many options for formatting this object, one of which is placement.

1 Display the **Format Legend** dialog box – double-click on the legend.

2 Open the **Placement** tab.

3 Choose a position for the legend.

4 Click **OK**.

Format Legend

| Patterns | Font | Placement |

Placement
- ○ Bottom
- ○ Corner
- ◉ Top
- ○ Right
- ○ Left

OK   Cancel

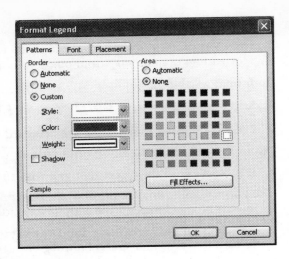

Explore the Patterns and Font tabs to see the other options for this object.

5.5 Scale

By default, the scale on a graph starts at 0. In many graphs, you may not have any low values, in which case you will have a large 'dead' area on your chart where no points are plotted. You could change the scaling at times like this, so that the graph starts at a value closer to the points that will be plotted.

1 Double-click on the axis to display the **Format Axis** dialog box for the Value axis.

2 Select the **Scale** tab.

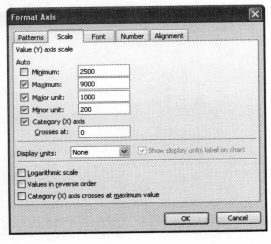

3 Set the **Minimum** value as required.

4 Click **OK**.

• Experiment with the other options in the dialog box.

5.6 Combination charts

You can combine chart types on some 2D charts. For example, you may want your chart to have most of the series displayed as a 2D column chart, but want one series displayed as a line to add interest, and make the series stand out from the others. Column, bar and line charts can be combined.

To combine a column and line chart:

1 Display your chart as a 2D column chart.

2 Select the series that you wish to display as a line – click on it.

3 Choose the **Line** option from the chart types displayed when you click the down arrow at the **Chart Type** tool.

• Format the line as required.

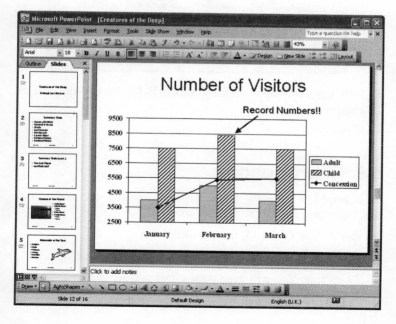

5.7 Overlap and gap width

The bars in a column or bar chart are displayed with no overlap between each series and a gap between each group. You can adjust the overlap and/or gap as required on your chart.

1 Display the **Format Data Series** dialog box – double-click on any data series.

2 Select the **Options** tab.

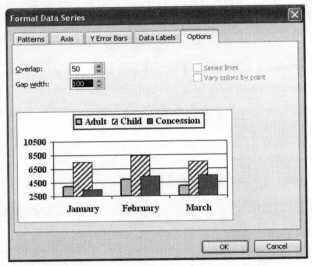

3 Edit the **Overlap** and **Gap width** fields to get the effects required.

4 Click **OK**.

5.8 Chart options

You should explore the Chart Options dialog box to find out what else you can do with your charts.

To display the Chart Options dialog box:

• Open the **Chart** menu and choose **Chart Options…**

• **Titles tab:** You can give your chart a title, or label the category and/or value axis on this tab.

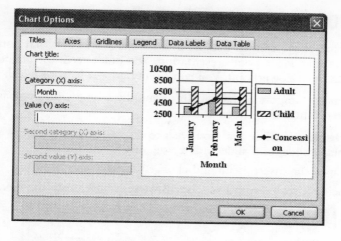

- **Axes:** Switch axes labels on or off, or customize the display of the category axes.

- **Gridlines:** Toggle the display of major and minor gridlines for either axis.

- **Legend:** You can switch the legend on or off, or control its position, from this tab.

- **Data Labels:** Choose data labels for your series. This one is particularly useful with pie charts.

- **Data Table:** You can switch the data table on and off from this tab, and toggle the display of the legend key.

5.9 Leaving Microsoft Graph

When your chart is complete, click anywhere on the slide outside the chart placeholder to return to your presentation.

The whole chart becomes an object within your presentation, and can be moved, copied, deleted or resized as necessary.

- To return to Microsoft Graph to edit a chart, simply double-click on the chart.

5.10 Importing a chart from Excel

You may have created a chart in an Excel workbook that you wish to include in your presentation. You don't need to recreate the chart in PowerPoint, you can simply import it from Excel.

When you import a chart in this way, the whole workbook is inserted into your presentation.

1 Display the slide that you wish to display your chart on – a blank slide, or a slide with a title only is fine for this.

2 Open the **Insert** menu and choose **Object**.

3 Select **Create From File**, click **Browse...** and locate the file.

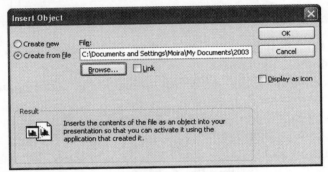

4 Click **OK** at the **Insert Object** dialog box.

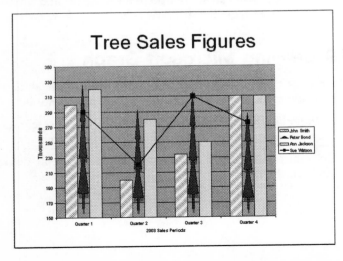

The whole workbook is inserted into your slide as an object. It is possible that the chart will not be visible, as it was not on the front-most sheet in the workbook.

If the chart you wish to display is not visible:

1 Double-click on the object to activate it.

2 Select the sheet tab that contains your chart.

3 Click outside the object to return to your presentation.

4 Move and/or resize the object as necessary.

Summary

In this chapter we have concentrated on creating charts on a slide. We have discussed:

+ Creating a chart in PowerPoint

+ Microsoft Graph toolbars and menus

+ Entering data onto the datasheet

+ Displaying data by row or by column

+ Hiding data

+ Number Formats

+ Chart types

+ Chart objects

+ Formatting chart objects

+ Scaling

+ Combination charts

+ Chart options

+ Importing charts from Excel

06

organization charts and diagrams

In this chapter you will learn:

- how to create organization charts
- how to create diagrams
- how to AutoFormat a diagram
- what animation effects can be used on charts

Aims of this chapter

This chapter introduces organization charts. We discuss creating them on your slides, adding and removing boxes, layout, scaling options, formatting and animation. This chapter also looks at other diagrams – cycle, radical, pyramid, Venn and target.

6.1 Organization charts

Creating an organization chart

There are three ways to set up an organization chart:

* Choose a layout with a **Diagram or Organization Chart** placeholder from the **Slide Layout** Task Pane.

Or

* Choose a layout with a **Content** placeholder from the **Slide Layout** Task Pane.

Or

* Click the **Insert Diagram or Organization Chart** tool.

To use the Diagram or Organization Chart placeholder:

1 Double-click in the placeholder on your slide.

2 Select **Organization Chart** from the **Diagram Gallery** dialog box.

3 Click **OK**.

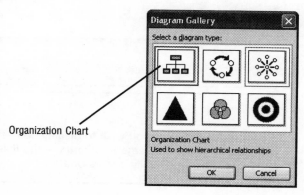

Organization Chart

To use a Contents placeholder:

1 Click the **Insert Diagram or Organization Chart** tool within the placeholder.

2 Select **Organization Chart** from the **Diagram Gallery** dialog box.

3 Click **OK**.

Insert Diagram or Organization Chart

To use a slide with no placeholder:

1 Click the **Insert Diagram or Organization Chart** tool 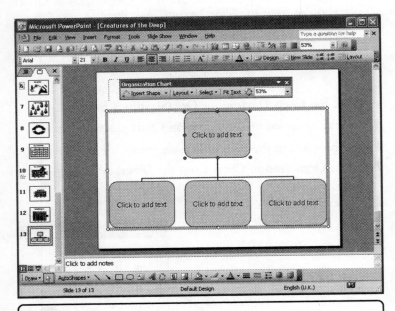 on the Drawing toolbar.

2 Select **Organization Chart** from the **Diagram Gallery** dialog box.

3 Click **OK**.

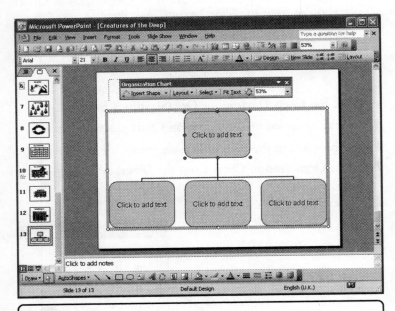

Tip

Work out the structure you wish to display before you start. Don't try to create too large a structure – the finished slide should be clear and easily understood.

An organization chart object will be displayed on the slide. You will see a set of boxes and the Organization Chart toolbar.

Entering text

1 Click in the box you wish to write in.

2 Key in your data.

3 Press [**Enter**] to create a new row if you have more than one line of data for the box.

4 Click on the next box to be completed, or outside the box, when you are finished.

Increase the Zoom percentage to get a close up of your text

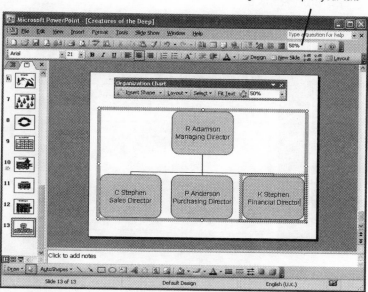

- If you click within the placeholder the Organization Chart toolbar remains visible. If you click outside it, the toolbar will disappear, but reappear when you click inside the Organization Chart placeholder again.

6.2 Adding and deleting boxes

You can build your chart up by adding boxes. Each new box must be related to an existing box. There are three types of relationship – subordinate, co-worker and assistant.

To add a box:

1 Click inside the box that you wish to relate a new box to.

2 Click the **Insert Shape** tool on the Organization Chart toolbar to insert a Subordinate box (the default).

Or

3 Click the drop-down arrow to the right of the **Insert Shape** tool and select the type of new box required.

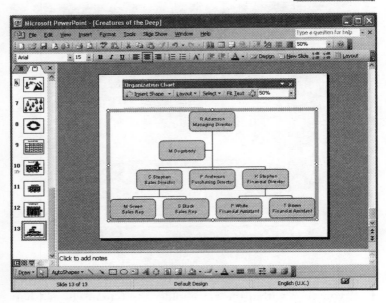

To delete a box:

1 Click in it, then click on its edge and press **[Delete]**.

• If you change your mind, click Undo 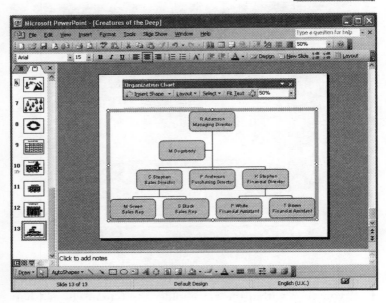 or press **[Ctrl]-[Z]** to undo the deletion.

6.3 Layout

There are a number of different layouts to choose from.

To change the layout:

1 Select a 'manager' box – one that has sub-ordinates.

2 Click the **Layout** button.

3 Select the layout option required.

Formatting the chart

You can AutoFormat the chart or format it manually, using the tools on the Formatting and Drawing toolbars.

To apply an AutoFormat to your chart:

1 Click the **AutoFormat** tool ▨ .

2 At the **Style Gallery,** select a Diagram Style and click **OK**.

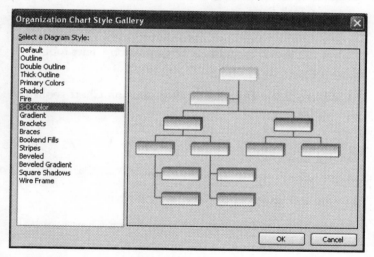

To format a box or a line:

1 Select the object – click on it.

2 Use the formatting tools on the Drawing toolbar, e.g. Line Style, Line Color, Fill, Shadow, etc.

To format text:

1 Select the text – drag over it.
2 Use the tools on the Formatting toolbar, e.g. Font size, Font color, Bold, Italic, etc.

6.4 Diagrams

Diagrams are used to represent conceptual data and to enliven your presentation.

You can add diagrams to your slides by creating a slide that has a Content placeholder on it, or by using the Insert Diagram or Organization Chart tool on the Drawing toolbar.

Creating a diagram

There are two main ways of creating a diagram:

• Choose a layout with a Content placeholder from the Slide Layout Task Pane.

Or

• Click the Insert Diagram or Organization Chart tool.

To use a Content placeholder:

1 Click the Insert Diagram or Organization Chart tool in the placeholder.

2 Select the diagram from the Diagram Gallery dialog box.
3 Click OK.   Insert Diagram or Organization Chart

To create a diagram where there is no placeholder:

1 Click the Insert Diagram or Organization Chart tool .
2 Select the diagram from the Diagram Gallery dialog box.
3 Click OK.
Follow the prompts on the slide to complete your diagram.

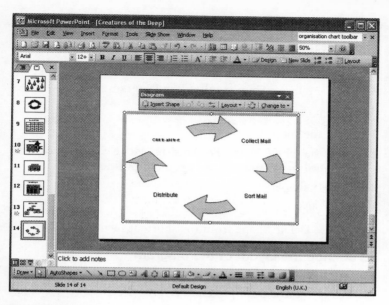

Diagram types

Cycle 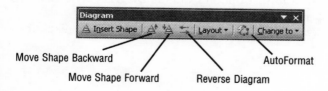 – used to show a process with a continuous cycle.

Radical – used to show relationships of a core element.

Pyramid – used to show foundation-based relationships.

Venn – used to show areas of overlap between elements.

Target – used to show steps towards a goal.

The Diagram toolbar is displayed when you are working on a diagram. Use it to help you set up and format your diagram.

Move Shape Backward

Move Shape Forward

Reverse Diagram

AutoFormat

Working with shapes

You can easily add more shapes to your diagram.

To add a shape:

• Click the **Insert Shape** tool on the Diagram toolbar.

To move a shape:

1 Select the shape.
2 Click the **Move Shape Forward** or **Move Shape Backward** tool until the shape is in the required position.

To delete a shape:

1 Right-click on it.
2 Choose **Delete Shape** from the shortcut menu.

To change the layout of the diagram

The Layout tool displays a number of options for controlling the size of the Diagram placeholder.

1 Click the **Layout** tool.
2 Select the option required from the drop-down list.

• Click **Fit Diagram to Contents** if you want the placeholder border to fit snugly around the diagram.

• Use **Expand Diagram** to add space around the diagram, within the placeholder.

• If you select **Resize Diagram,** resize handles appear in the corners and along the edges of the placeholder. Click and drag the handles to resize the diagram as required.

AutoFormat

AutoFormats can add impact to a diagram.

1 Click the **AutoFormat** tool .
2 Choose a format option from the **Diagram Style Gallery**.
3 Click **OK**.

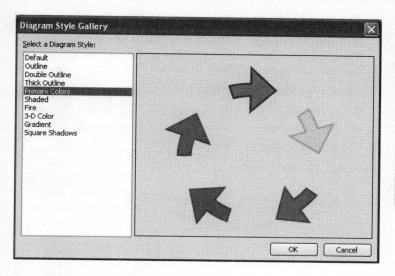

Changing the diagram type

If you decide that you would rather use a different type for your diagram, you can always change it.

1 Click the **Change To...** tool on the Diagram toolbar.
2 Select the diagram type required from the list.

6.5 Animation

Animation can be used to create greater visual impact when your slide is displayed in a presentation.

To animate your chart:

1 Open the **Slide Show** menu.
2 Choose **Custom Animation...**
3 The Custom Animation Task Pane will appear. Select the Organization Chart (if necessary).
4 Click **Add Effect...**
5 Choose the effect that you wish to use from the list.

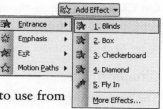

- Numbered tabs appear on the slide in Normal view when the Custom Animation Task Pane is displayed. These indicate the order in which the animation will be carried out. The tabs do not appear in Slide Sorter or Slide Show view.

To change the animation effect:

1 Select the effect in the animation list on the Task Pane.

2 Click the **Change** button.

3 Select the effect required.

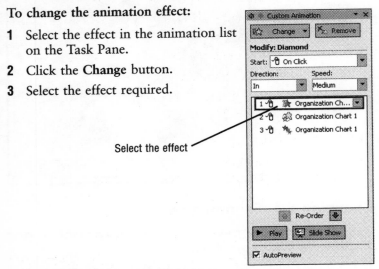

Select the effect

Customizing the animation

Once you have added an effect, you can use the fields in the **Custom Animation** Task Pane to customize the way the effect is executed.

Start

This option sets when the animation effect will start. There are three options – **On Click** (the one you are most likely to want), **With Previous** or **After Previous**.

On Click   Starts the animation when you click the mouse.

With Previous   Starts at the same time as the previous item.

After Previous   Starts after the previous item has finished.

Direction

The options vary, depending on the animation selected.

Speed

Select the speed that you think is best for your diagram.

Effect Options

You can further customize the effects from the **Effect Options** dialog box.

1 Right-click on the animation effect on the Task Pane.

2 Left-click on **Effect Options**.

3 Explore the **Effect, Timing** and **Diagram Animation** tabs to see what options are available.

Diagram Animation

You can create a build effect for your chart from the Diagram Animation tab in the Effect Options dialog box.

1 Click the drop-down arrow on the animation effect on the Task Pane.

2 Left-click on **Effect Options**.

3 Select the **Diagram Animation** tab.

4 Choose the option required from the **Group diagram** list.

5 Click **OK**.

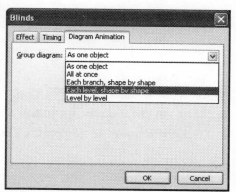

You can also customize the animation effect on each object within your chart – but be careful not to overdo things. Just because it is possible, doesn't necessarily mean that it is a good thing.

You must group the diagram using an option other than *As one object*, if you wish to customize the effects on individual objects.

To customize the effects on individual boxes:

1 Click the **Expand contents** bar to list the different boxes in your chart.

2 Click the drop-down arrow on the box that you wish to customize.

3 Choose **Effect Options...** from the list.

4 Customize the options as required.

♦ Scroll to the bottom of the contents list and click the **Hide Contents** bar to collapse the contents list again.

To remove an animation effect:

1 Select the effect on the list in the Task Pane.

2 Click the **Remove** button on the Task Pane.

Summary

In this chapter we have looked at organization charts and diagrams. We have discussed:

- Creating organization charts
- Adding and removing boxes
- Changing the layout of organization charts
- Formatting organization charts
- Creating diagrams – cycle, radical, pyramid, Venn and target
- Inserting, moving and deleting shapes
- Changing a diagram layout
- AutoFormatting diagrams
- Changing a diagram type
- Animation in charts and diagrams

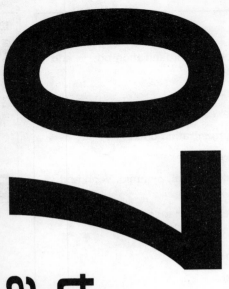

07

tables, clip art and sound

In this chapter you will learn:

- how to create tables
- some ways of manipulating and formatting your tables
- about inserting and formatting clip art
- how to add sound effects

Aims of this chapter

In this chapter we will consider the use of tables, pictures and sounds on slides. Tables can display data in columns and rows. Pictures add interest to your slides, and sounds can help focus your audience's attention on specific points.

7.1 Tables

If you have created tables in Word, you'll find it very easy to create them on slides. A table is inserted as an object and can be created in several ways. You can:

♦ Create a new slide with a **Table** placeholder set up.

♦ Create a new slide with a **Content** placeholder.

♦ *Draw* your table onto your slide.

♦ Use the **Insert Table** tool on the Standard toolbar.

To start from a slide with Table placeholder:

1 Double-click on the **Table** placeholder on your slide.

2 Set the number of columns and rows.

3 Click **OK**.

To start from a slide with a Content placeholder:

1 Click the **Insert Table** tool within the placeholder.

2 Specify the number of columns and rows required.

3 Click **OK**.

The Tables and Borders toolbar

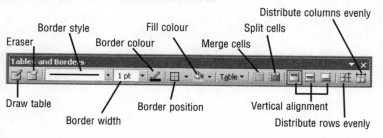

Distribute columns evenly
Border style
Fill colour
Split cells
Eraser
Border colour
Merge cells
Draw table
Border position
Vertical alignment
Border width
Distribute rows evenly

To draw a table:

1   Click the **Tables and Borders** tool ▧ on the Standard toolbar to display the Tables and Borders toolbar.

2   The **Draw Table** tool ▧ is automatically selected (if you had the Tables and Borders toolbar displayed already, click the **Draw Table** tool to select it).

3   Click and drag on your slide to draw a rectangle the size you want your table to be.

4   Draw in rows and columns where you want them.

5   Switch the **Draw Table** tool off – click ▧ or press [**Esc**].

If you draw a line in the wrong place, remove it with the **Eraser** – select the tool ▧, then click on the line you wish to erase with the tip of the Eraser.

To draw a table on a slide with no placeholder:

1   Click on the **Insert Table** tool on the Standard toolbar.

2   Click and drag over the grid to specify the table size required.

4 x 3 Table

To move around in a table:

♦   Press [**Tab**] to move to the next cell.

♦   Press [**Shift**]-[**Tab**] to go to the previous cell.

Or

♦   Use the arrow keys to move up, down, right and left.

Or

♦   Click in the cell you wish to work on.

Click outside your table when you've finished working on it (the Tables and Borders toolbar will disappear).

♦   Use the Formatting and Tables and Borders toolbars to format your data.

Number of Visitors

	January	February	March
Adult	4000	5000	4000
Child	7500	8400	7500
Concession	3500	5400	5500

Tips when working with tables

- To select table cells: drag over them.
- To adjust a column width: drag the left column border.
- To adjust a row height: drag the lower row border.
- To insert or delete a row or column: click the **Table** button on the Tables and Borders toolbar, and select the option. (You will then need to adjust the column width/row height manually to get a good fit).

- To resize rows or columns so that they are the same height/width, select them, then use the **Distribute Rows Evenly** or **Distribute Columns Evenly** tools.

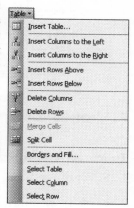

Experiment with the table formatting options.

To merge cells:

1 Select the cells that are to be merged.

2 Click the **Merge Cells** tool 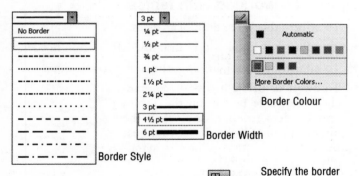.

To split cells:

1 Select the cell that is to be split.

2 Click the **Split Cell** tool .

To format the border style, width or colour:

1 Select the cells.

2 Select the style from the drop-down list.

Or

◆ Select the width from the drop-down list.

Or

◆ Choose the colour from the drop-down palette.

Border Style

Border Width

Border Colour

Specify the border

3 Specify the border position.

To set the vertical alignment:

1 Select the cells.

2 Click an alignment tool to set the alignment.

Using the Format Table dialog box

You can also format your table from the **Format Table** dialog box.

To display the dialog box:

1 Select the cells that you want to format.

2 Open the **Format** menu and choose **Table...**

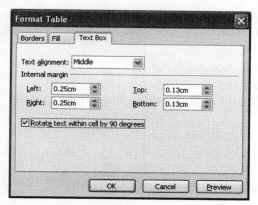

3 Explore the tabs.

The **Borders** and **Fill** tabs have little more than is available on the toolbar, but the Text Box tab has one or two additional features, including text rotation.

7.2 Clip Art

Office comes with hudreds of clip art pictures that can be added to slides. You can also find many more clips on the Internet.

There are four main ways of getting your hands (or mouse) on the clip art.

◆ Set up a New Slide with a **Clip Art** placeholder on it.

◆ Choose a layout from the **Slide Layout** Task Pane that has a Content placeholder already on it.

◆ Click the **Insert Clip Art** tool ▨ on the Drawing toolbar.

◆ Insert from the Clip Organizer.

From a slide with a Clip Art placeholder:

• Double click within the Clip Art placeholder.

Insert Clip Art

From a slide with a Content placeholder:

• Click the **Insert Clip Art** tool in the placeholder.

Both of these options take you to the Select Picture dialog box. (Connect to the Internet to get access to even more pictures.)

To select a picture:

1 Scroll through the pictures, and then select the one that you want and click **OK**.

Or

2 Enter a keyword into the **Search text** field and click **Go**.

3 Select the picture that you want to use and click **OK**.

From a slide with no placeholder set:

1 Click the **Insert Clip Art** tool 🖾 on the Drawing toolbar.

2 At the Clip Art Task Pane, enter a keyword, e.g. *animal* in the **Search text:** field.

3 Set your search options.

4 Click **Go**.

• If you don't enter a keyword, all available clips are displayed.

5 If you don't find anything suitable, try another keyword (or leave the **Search text:** field empty, and scroll through all the clips to see what is available).

6 Double-click on a clip to insert it.

7.3 Clip Art on Office Online

If you have access to the Internet you will find hundreds of clips online. Click **Clip Art on Office Online** at the bottom of the Clip Art Task pane and explore the online clips.

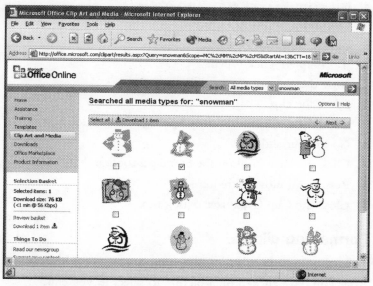

To search for a clip:

1 Specify your search options in the **Search** field.

2 Click 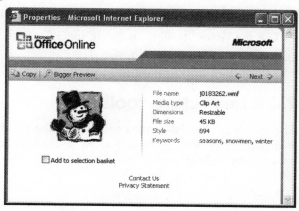.

3 Move through the pages using the right/left arrows – click on a clip to preview it.

4 Select the clips required – select the checkbox under the clip.

5 Click the **Download** button once you've selected your clips.

6 If the **Office Media & Template Control** screen appears, click **Continue**.

7 Click **Download Now**.

8 If prompted, click **Open**.

To copy the clip onto your slide:

1 Select the clip.

2 Click the **Copy** tool in the **Clip Organizer** dialog box.

3 Go to your slide.

4 Click the **Paste** tool on the Standard toolbar.

5 Resize and move as required.

6 Close the **Clip Organizer** dialog box.

Formatting clips

The picture can be edited in the same way as other objects.

After you have clicked on a picture to select it, you can...

- Press [**Delete**] to delete the object.
- Click and drag any of the handles around the edges of the picture to resize it.
- Click and drag within the picture (not a handle) to move it.
- Use the **Picture** toolbar to create special effects.

Deselect it by clicking anywhere off it.

7.4 The Picture toolbar

The clips that you insert into your document can be formatted in a number of ways – the best thing to do is experiment with the options and see what effect they have.

When a clip is selected the Picture toolbar is displayed. You can use the toolbar to modify your picture.

Working from left to right on the toolbar:

◆ **Insert Picture** – Inserts a picture *from File* rather than from the **Clip Organizer** or **Select Picture** dialog box.

◆ **Color** – *Automatic* is the default. *Grayscale* converts each colour to a different shade of grey. *Black and white* converts the picture to a black and white picture. *Watermark* converts the object to a low contrast picture that you can place behind everything else to create a watermark.

◆ **More Contrast** – Increase the contrast.

◆ **Less Contrast** – Decrease the contrast.

◆ **More Brightness** – Increase the brightness.

◆ **Less Brightness** – Decrease the brightness.

◆ **Crop** – Lets you trim the edges of the clip.

To crop a clip:

1 Select it.

2 Click the **Crop** tool.

3 Drag a resizing handle to crop (cut off) the bits you don't want.

◆ **Rotate Left** – Rotates the object 90° to the left.

◆ **Line Style** – Use to put lines around the picture, or change the line style used.

◆ **Compress Pictures** – Displays a dialog box which displays options for reducing the picture's file size.

◆ **Recolor picture** – Displays a dialog box where you can change the colours used in a picture.

◆ **Format Picture** – Opens the Format Picture dialog box where you have access to even more formatting options.

◆ **Set Transparent Color** – Used to create a transparent colour in a picture on your page. This will work with bitmaps, JPEGs and GIFs that don't have transparency information, and also some – but not all – clip art. It does not work with animated GIFs.

+ **Reset Picture** – returns the clip to its original state.

7.5 Sound

You can add sound to your slides from the Media Clip dialog box or the Clip Organizer.

To add sound from the Media Clip dialog box:

1 Create a layout with a Media Clip or a **Content** placeholder.

2 Double-click the **Media Clip** placeholder.

Or

+ Click the **Insert Media Clip** tool in the **Content** placeholder.

3 Select the clip you wish to add (sound or video clip).

4 Click **OK**.

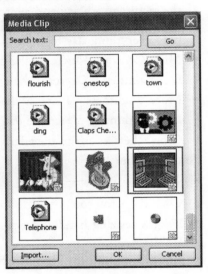

To add a sound from the Clip Organizer:

1 Display the **Clip Organizer** dialog box.

2 Locate a folder that contains sounds.

3 Select the sound.

4 Right-click on the drop-down arrow to the right of the clip.

5 Select **Copy**.

6 Return to your slide.

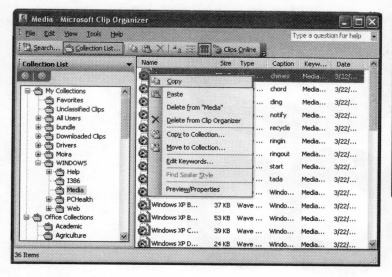

7 Paste the clip in.

8 Move/resize the clip as required.

♦ When giving a slide show, click on the sound icon to play it.

Summary

In this chapter we have discussed:

♦ Tables for displaying columns and rows of data

♦ Clip art to illustrate a point or add interest to a slide

♦ Sound – don't overdo this – but it can be effective!

08

masters

In this chapter you will learn:

- about the masters for slides, title slides, handouts and notes
- how to delete and restore placeholders on masters

Aims of this chapter

This chapter discusses Masters. Each presentation is based on a design template which consists of a slide master, title master (optional), and the various styles for the presentation, e.g. font styles, placeholder sizes and positions, background design, colour scheme, etc. Masters are used as the pattern for the slides in your presentation. If you wish to make a layout or formatting change that will be reflected on all slides (or all title slides), you should update the appropriate master. There are also masters for handouts and notes pages.

8.1 Slide Master

A Slide Master is added to a presentation any time you apply a design template. Most design templates have a Slide Master and a Title Master – the Slide–Title Master pair. These are displayed as miniatures in the slide panel when you view a master.

Any background objects you want to appear on every slide (e.g. a company name or logo) should be added to the Slide Master.

Changes to the Slide Master will be reflected in every slide in your presentation (except the Title Slide). Any slides where you have made changes to the text formatting at slide level will be treated as exceptions and will retain their custom formatting.

To access the master slides:

1 Choose **Master** from the **View** menu.

2 Select **Slide Master**.

3 Amend the Slide Master as required (using the same techniques you use on a slide in your presentation).

4 Click the **Close Master View** tool, or choose an alternative view, to leave your Slide Master.

♦ If you hold down [**Shift**] and click the **Normal View** icon, this takes you to the Slide Master or to the Title Master if you are on the title slide at the time.

♦ The title slide has its own master. Changes made to the Slide Master will not be reflected on your Title slide.

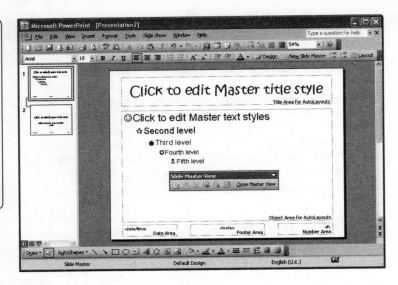

The Slide Master View toolbar

From left to right:

- **Insert New Slide Master** adds a new Slide Master to your presentation – each presentation must have at least one Slide Master.

- **Insert New Title Master** adds a new Title Master to your presentation.

- **Delete Master** deletes the selected Master.

- **Preserve Master** protects the Master from being deleted automatically by PowerPoint.

When all the slides that follow a master are deleted, or when another template is applied to all the slides that follow a master, PowerPoint usually automatically deletes the Slide Master. You can 'preserve' a Master so it isn't automatically deleted.

To preserve a Master:

- Click the **Preserve Master** tool. (If you change your mind, click it again toggle the preserve status off.)

Note that a master can be deleted manually even when it has a 'preserved' setting.

• **Rename Master** opens a dialog box where you can rename the Master.

• **Master Layout** displays the Master Layout dialog box, where you can switch on any placeholders that you have deleted from the master.

• **Close Master View** returns you to the view you were in before accessing the Masters.

The placeholders

The Object Areas for AutoLayouts, Date Area, Footer Area or Number Area placeholders are all optional. They can easily be deleted – or put back if you decide you want them after all.

You can delete any of the master placeholders – if you don't want to use them.

To delete placeholder:

• Select the placeholder and press [**Delete**].

To restore placeholders:

1 Click the **Master Layout** tool  on the Slide Master View toolbar.

2 Select the placeholders required.

3 Click **OK**.

Multiple Masters

If a presentation uses more than one design template, e.g. a different template for different sections of the presentation, you will have more than one set of masters. The Slide Master toolbar has a set of tools that can be used when working with multiple slide masters – tools for adding, deleting, renaming and preserving slide masters.

If you want to prevent multiple masters being used in a presentation, you can disable the feature in the Options dialog box.

To toggle the Enable Multiple Masters option:

1 Open the **Tools** menu and choose **Options...**

2 Select the **Edit** tab.

3 Under the **Disable new features** options, select or deselect the **Multiple masters** checkbox.

4 Click **OK**.

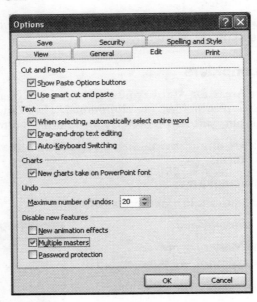

8.2 Notes Master

Each slide in your presentation has an accompanying notes page which consists of a smaller version of the slide along with room for any notes you want to make.

If you want to add information to your notes pages (company name or page number perhaps), or change the size of the placeholders (to allow more space for notes and less for the slide image) do so on the Notes Master.

1 Choose **Master** from the **View** menu.

2 Select **Notes Master**.

3 Amend the Notes Master as required.

4 Click **Close Master View** or choose an alternative view to leave your Notes Master.

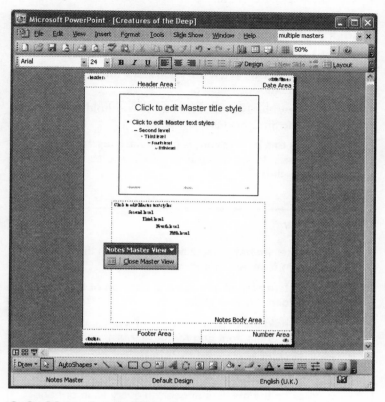

8.3 Handout Master

You can support your presentation with audience handouts if you wish. Handouts consist of smaller, printed versions of your slides, 1, 2, 3, 4, 6 or 9 to the page.

If you want additional information on each handout page, e.g. your company name or logo, the presentation title, page numbers or date, you can add the detail to the Handout Master.

To edit the Handout Master:

1 Choose **Master** from the **View** menu.

2 Select **Handout Master**.

3 Select 1, 2, 3, 6 or 9 slides to the page.

4 Edit the Master as required.

5 To edit the header and/or footer choose **Header and Footer** from the **View** menu and select the **Notes and Handouts** tab.

6 Edit the header and/or footer text and click **Apply to All**.

7 Click **Close Master View** or choose an alternative view to leave your Handout Master.

• You can view the Handout Master if you hold down **[Shift]** and click the Slide Sorter View icon.

• The 3 slides to a page layout is particularly useful if you want to leave space for your audience to make their own notes beside each slide.

Summary

In this chapter we have discussed the masters that are part of the design template of a presentation.

• The masters control the size and position of the default placeholders on your slides

• Masters hold the design elements of a presentation, e.g. colour schemes, font and font size, bullet style, etc.

• Global changes to slides should be made on the slide master, and to title slides on the title slide master

• Objects on the masters appear on every slide or page

• The masters can be displayed by holding down [Shift] when you click a View icon

09

slide show preparation

In this chapter you will learn:

- how to prepare a slide show
- how to create notes
- about transitions and animation
- how to create a summary slide
- some ways of customizing the show setup

Aims of this chapter

In this chapter we will look at a number of features that can enhnce your presentation, including:

- Hiding slides
- Producing speaker notes
- Setting up transitions and animations on slides
- Producing a summary slide
- Rehearsing timings
- Creating a custom show

9.1 Slide show tools

The topics introduced in this section are useful if you will be giving on-screen presentations (a slide show). They do not apply to overheads and 35mm slides.

- Transitions, Text Animation and Hiding Slides can be specified in any view using the Tools menu, but I find it easiest to do them from Slide Sorter view using the Slide Sorter toolbar.

Slide Sorter toolbar

Hide Slide

This option can prove useful if you're not sure whether or not you will really need a particular slide for your presentation. You can include the slide in your presentation (in case it's needed), but hide it. The hidden slide will be bypassed during your slide show, unless you decide you need to use it.

To hide a slide:

1 Select the slide you want to hide.

2 Click the **Hide Slide** tool ▦.

- The number is crossed out under the slide.
- If you want to show the hidden slide during a presentation press [H] at the slide preceding the hidden one.

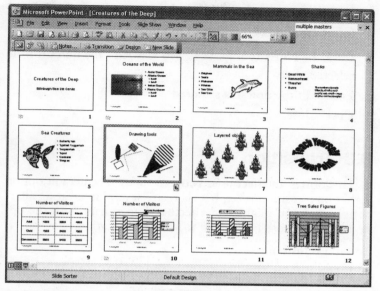

- To remove the hidden status from a slide, select it and click the **Hide Slide** tool ⊞ again.

9.2 Notes

If you are giving the presentation, you will probably find Notes useful. You can print your notes out, and use them to prompt you during your talk.

To enter and edit Notes:

1 Click in the **Notes** Pane in Normal view.

2 Type and edit your notes.

Or

1 Open the **View** menu and choose **Notes Page**.

2 Click in the Notes area and type in your notes.

(You may want to increase the Zoom if you enter notes in this view, so that you can read your text.)

You can also input and edit your notes in Slide Show view. This option may be particularly useful when you are practising a show.

1 Select the slide that you wish to update the notes of.

2 Click the **Notes** tool 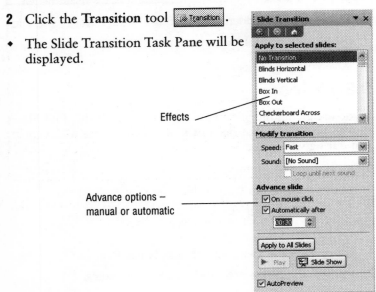 to view/edit the notes for the selected slide.

3 Enter/edit the notes as required.

4 Click **Close**.

9.3 Transition

A transition is an effect used between slides. The default option is that no transition is set, but there are several interesting alternatives that you might find effective. Experiment with the options to find those best suited to your presentation.

To set a transition:

1 Select the slide(s) to which you want to specify a transition.

2 Click the **Transition** tool .

• The Slide Transition Task Pane will be displayed.

Effects

Advance options – manual or automatic

Slide Transition

Apply to selected slides:

No Transition
Blinds Horizontal
Blinds Vertical
Box In
Box Out
Checkerboard Across
Checkerboard Down

Modify transition

Speed: Fast

Sound: [No Sound]

Loop until next sound

Advance slide

☑ On mouse click
☑ Automatically after
30:30

Apply to All Slides

► Play Slide Show

☑ AutoPreview

3 Select the effect required from the list (it will be previewed if **AutoPreview** is selected at the bottom of the Task Pane).

4 Set the **Speed** to *Fast*. Focus your audiences on your slides, not the transition method!

5 Select a **Sound** if you wish.

6 Choose an **Advance** option.

Other options:

+ **Apply to All** applies the effect to all slides in the presentation, not just the one(s) you have selected. New slides will not have the transition effect.

+ **Play** previews the effect on the selected slide.

+ **Slide Show** displays the slide and effect in Slide Show view.

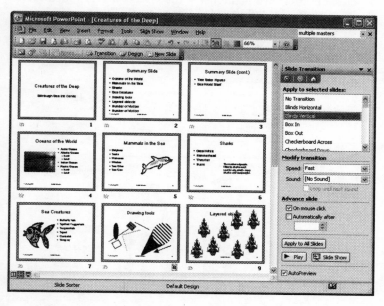

If a transition is set, a transition icon ⌣ appears below the slide in Slide Sorter view. Click on it to see the effect.

9.4 Animation

If you have several points listed in the body text of your slide, you could try building the slide up during the presentation, rather than presenting the whole list at once. Experiment with the Animation options and effects until you find the ones you prefer. You can have a lot of fun messing about with the options – but try to avoid having a different effect on each slide!

To set an animation effect:

1 Click the **Design** tool 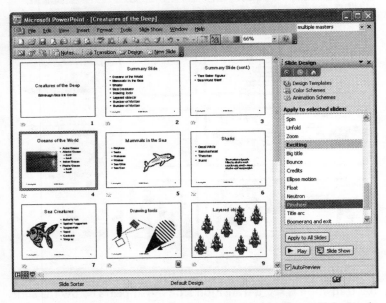 to display the Design Task Pane.
2 Select **Animation Schemes** on the Slide Design Task Pane.
3 Select the slide(s) that you wish to animate.
4 Pick an effect from the list – the effects are grouped under *Recently Used, Subtle, Moderate* and *Exciting*.

• If you want all the slides to have the same effect, click **Apply to All Slides**.
5 Close the Pane when you have specified your requirements.

To check the effect at full screen:

* Select the slide, then click the **Slide Show icon** 🖳, work through your slide then press **[Esc]** to return to Slide Sorter view.

Custom animations

You can set up your own animations (rather than use the preset ones) if you wish. You must be in Normal view for this to work.

1 Go into **Normal view**.

2 Display the slide that you wish to animate.

3 Open the **Slide Show** menu and choose **Custom Animation**.

4 Select the object on your slide that you wish to animate.

5 Click the **Add Effect** button (or **Change** if the object is already animated), and choose an effect from the options listed.

6 Specify the **Start**, and other options – these vary depending on the effect chosen.

To customize the animation of an item:

1 Click the drop-down arrow to the right of the object name.

2 Select **Effect Options...**

3 Open the Effect, Timing or Text Animation tab.

4 Specify the options as required.

5 Click **OK**.

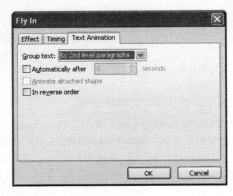

9.5 Summary slide

You can get PowerPoint to automatically produce a summary slide for your presentation. This will be placed in front of the other slides, and list the titles of each selected slide.

To create a summary slide:

1 Hold [**Shift**] and click to select the slides from which you wish to produce a summary slide.

2 Click the **Summary Slide** tool 🔲 on the Slide Sorter toolbar.

• PowerPoint will generate as many summary slides as are needed to list the title detail from all the slides you select.

9.6 Rehearse timings

It is a very good idea to practise your presentation before you end up in front of your audience. As well as practising what you intend to say (probably with the aid of notes you have made using the Notes Page feature), you can rehearse the timings for each slide.

1 Click the **Rehearse Timings** tool 🔲 to go into your slide show for a practice run.

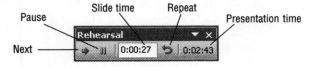

2 Go over what you intend to say while the slide is displayed.

3 Click the left mouse button to move to the next slide when ready.

4 Repeat steps 2 and 3 until you reach the end of your presentation.

Displaying timings

A dialog box displays the total length of time your presentation took and asks if you want to record and use the new slide timings in a slide show. Choose **Yes**, if you want each slide to advance after the allocated time.

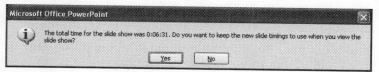

The slide timings will be displayed in Slide Sorter view.

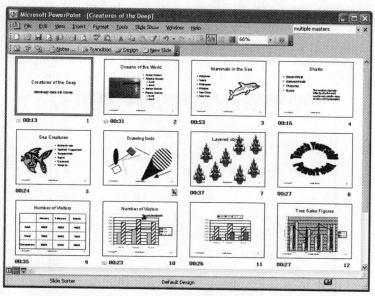

* You can rehearse your timings as often as is necessary, until you've got the pace right to get your message across.

- You can set timings manually in the Slide Transition Task Pane. Click the **Transition** tool 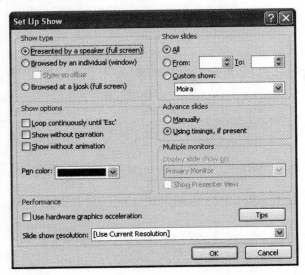 to display it (see section 9.3).

9.7 Set Up Show

A slide show can be presented in a number of different ways:

- By a presenter
- Driven by the audience
- Automatically.

You may want to use all the slides in your presentation, or a subset of them.

You might want the slide show to run in a continuous loop, or you could choose to use or not use animation effects that you have set up.

The slides can be set to advance manually (when you click the mouse) or by using slide timings if you have saved them.

By default, a slide show is assumed to be presenter driven, with all slides used. Animation effects will run and the show will progress manually – when the presenter clicks the mouse.

However, if you wish your slide show to be controlled using either of the other methods (perhaps for an open day, or at a sales event), or if you wish to change any of the default settings, you can easily change the set up options.

To specify the slide show set up:

1 Open the **Slide Show** menu.

2 Select **Set Up Show**.

3 Specify the options required and click **OK**.

9.8 Custom Show

You can quickly set up a custom show from the slides that you have in your presentation if you wish. This could be useful if you have a number of slides in your presentation, but wish to be able to 'mix and match' them for different audiences.

To create a custom show:

1 Open the **Slide Show** menu.

2 Choose **Custom Shows...**

3 Click **New...**

4 At the **Define Custom Show** dialog box, give your show a name.

To add slides to the custom show:

1 Select the first slide you require from the list on the left.

2 Click **Add >>** to add it to your show.

3 Repeat until all slides have been added.

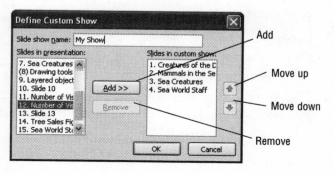

To remove slides from the custom show:

1 Select the slide you wish to remove from the list on the right.

2 Click **Remove**.

To move slides within the custom show:

1 Select the slide you wish to move in the list on the right.

2 Click the **Move Up** and **Move Down** button as necessary.

When you are done, click **OK** to close the **Define Custom Show** dialog box, then click **Close** at the **Custom Shows** dialog box.

To edit a custom show:

1 Open the **Slide Show** menu.

2 Choose **Custom Shows...**

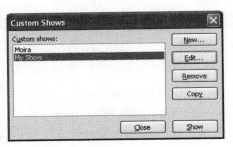

3 Select the show that you wish to edit.

4 Click **Edit...**

5 Add, remove or move slides as required.

6 Click **OK**.

To delete a custom show:

1 Open the **Slide Show** menu.

2 Choose **Custom Shows...**

3 Select the show you wish to delete.

4 Click **Remove**.

To copy a custom show:

1 Open the **Slide Show** menu.

2 Choose **Custom Shows...**

3 Select the show you wish to copy.

4 Click **Copy**.

5 Edit the copy as required.

To show a custom show:

1 Open the **Slide Show** menu.
2 Choose **Custom Shows...**
3 Select the show you wish to run.
4 Click **Show**.

Summary

In this chapter we have discussed some of the features that you can use to add the finishing touches to your presentation in preparation for your actual slide show.

We have looked at:

- Hiding slides that you may not want to use in your main presentation, but keep them easily accessible should you require them

- Speaker Notes

- Adding transitions to add impact as your slides appear during a slide show

- Animation schemes to gradually build up the main points on your slide

- Adding a summary slide to your presentation

- Practising your presentation with the Rehearse Timings tool

- The Set Up options for your slide show

- Creating Custom Shows

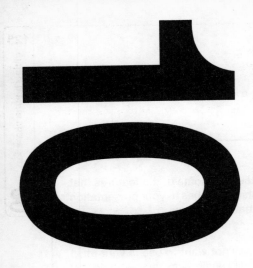

10

giving a slide show

In this chapter you will learn:

- how to run your slide show
- some ways of working with your slide show
- about PowerPoint viewer
- how to save your file in different formats

Aims of this chapter

In this chapter we will discuss the basic skills required to run a slide show, and some of the features that are available to you when delivering your presentation. These are useful when the presentation is presented by a speaker (rather than run automatically).

10.1 Running a slide show

You can run a slide show at any time to check how the presentation is progressing. Each slide fills the whole of the screen. After the last, you are returned to the view you were in when you clicked the **Slide Show** tool.

1 Select the slide you want to start from, usually the first.

2 Click the **Slide Show** (from current slide) icon 🖳 to the left of the horizontal scroll bar.

3 Work through your presentation.

To move forward to the next slide:

♦ Click the **Next** arrow 🔲 on the Slide Show toolbar.

Or

♦ Click the left mouse button.

Or

♦ Press [**PageDown**].

To move back to the previous slide:

♦ Click the Previous arrow 🔲 on the Slide Show toolbar.

Or

♦ Press [**PageUp**].

To exit your slide show:

♦ Press [**Esc**].

Use the Slide Show along with Slide Sorter view when experimenting with Transition and Animation. Then you can check that the options you choose are having the desired effect.

Working within your slide show

When presenting your show, you might want to leave the normal sequence, go directly to a slide or draw on the slide to focus attention. These and other features can be accessed using the pop-up menu or the keyboard.

1   Click the pop-up menu icon ▦ at the bottom left of the screen.

To go directly to a slide:

2   Select **Go to Slide**.

3   Click on the slide you want to go to.

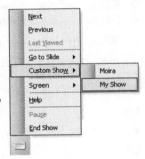

To run a Custom Show from a slide show:

1   Display the pop-up menu.

2   Select **Custom Show**.

3   Click on the show that you wish to run.

10.2 Slide show options

Blackout and whiteout

Sometimes, you might like to blackout or whiteout the screen so as not to distract your audience as you demonstrate something.

To blackout your screen:

♦   Press [B].

To whiteout your screen:

♦   Press [W].

Press [B] or [W] again to return to your slide show.

Pens and arrows

You can change your pointer to a *pen* so that you can annotate a slide, or draw something on your 'blackboard' or 'whiteboard'.

To display the pen options:

* Click the **Pen** tool [ ] on the Slide Show toolbar at the bottom left of the screen.

To select a colour and pen style:

1 Select the pen colour required from the **Ink Color** options.

2 Choose the Pen style required – ballpoint, felt tip or highlighter.

3 Drag on your slide.

To erase the ink on your slide:

1 Click the **Pen** tool.

2 Choose **Eraser**, then click on the annotation that you wish to remove.

Or

* Click **Erase All Ink on Slide**.

You can also use keyboard shortcuts to switch between the pointer and pen, and to erase all of the ink on your slide.

* To change the mouse pointer to a pen, press **[Ctrl]-[P]**.

* To change the mouse pointer to an arrow, press **[Ctrl]-[A]**.

* To erase all of your ink, press **[Ctrl]-[E]**.

At the end of your slide show, you will be given the opportunity to keep or discard any ink annotations that you have made.

* Click **Keep** to preserve them, or **Discard** to erase them.

10.3 Slide Show Help

Slide Shows have a Slide Show Help dialog box that can be displayed when a show is running. This may be useful when you are practising your presentation, and learning about the options.

To display the Slide Show Help dialog box:

1 Press [F1].

2 Experiment with the options, and use any that you find useful during your shows.

3 Click **OK** to close the **Slide Show Help** dialog box.

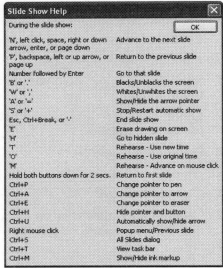

10.4 PowerPoint Viewer

There may be times that you need to give a presentation on another computer, which does not have Microsoft PowerPoint on it. You can use the PowerPoint Viewer to package your presentation so that it can be viewed on the computer.

To package your presentation:

1 Open the presentation.

2 Choose **Package for CD...** from the **File** menu.

3 Edit the CD name if required.

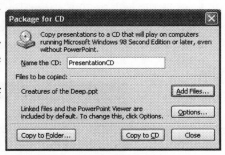

4 If you have more files to add, click **Add Files...** and select the files required.

5 If you want to change the packaging options click **Options** and amend as necessary.

6 Click **Copy to CD**.

7 Close the dialog box.

To view the presentation using PowerPoint Viewer:

1 Display the contents of the CD.

2 Double-click **Pptview.exe**.

3 Select the presentation that you want to view.

4 Click **Open**.

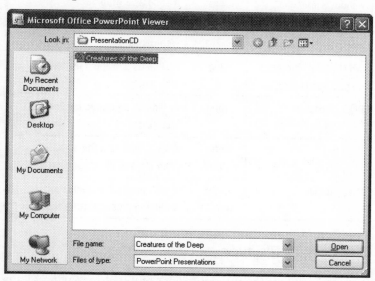

10.5 File formats

When you save a presentation in the default file format it is saved as a PowerPoint Presentation File. You can choose from a variety of file types, depending on your requirements. You may need to use a different file format if your presentation will be run on an earlier version of PowerPoint or on the Internet. The main file types are summarized on the following page.

File type	Extension	Use to save
Presentation	.ppt	A normal PowerPoint presentation
Design template	.pot	Presentation as a template
PowerPoint show	.pps	A presentation that will open as a slide show
PowerPoint 97-2003 and 95 presentation	.ppt	Files that must be opened by previous versions
Outline/RTF	.rtf	A presentation outline as an outline document
Windows metafile	.wmf	A slide as a graphic
GIF (Graphics Interchange Format)	.gif	A slide as a graphic for use on web pages
JPEG (Joint Photographics Experts Group)	.jpg	A slide as a graphic for use on web pages
PNG (Portable Network Graphics)	.png	A slide as a graphic for use on web pages
Web page	.htm .html	A web page as a folder with an .htm file and all supporting files
Web archive	.mht .mhtml	A web page as a single file including all supporting files

The default file type

It is assumed that the normal format required for saving files is the current default PowerPoint Presentation. If you wish to specify a different default, you can do so in the Options dialog box.

To choose a default file type for saving your presentations:

1 Open the **Tools** menu and choose **Options...**

2 Select the **Save** tab.

3 Choose the format required from the **Save PowerPoint files as:** list.

4 Click **OK**.

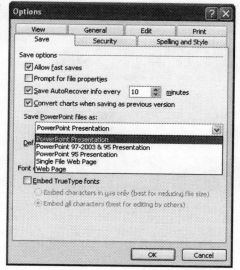

Summary

In this chapter we have considered:

* The skills needed to run your slide show
* Slide navigation during a show
* Running a Custom Show
* Slide show options, e.g. blackouts, whiteouts, pens and arrows
* PowerPoint Viewer
* Saving your presentation in different formats

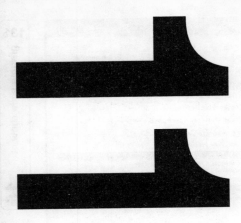

14

printing
presentations

In this chapter you will learn:

- how to set up your presentation for printing
- how to specify what you want printed
- how to print a selection of slides

Aims of this chapter

This chapter discusses the print options available for your presentation. You can print your whole presentation in PowerPoint – the slides, speaker notes, audience handouts and the presentation outline. You can print copies of your slides onto paper or onto overhead transparencies, or you could get a bureau to create the slides for you.

11.1 Page setup

The first stage to printing your presentation is to specify the slide setup. You set the slide size and orientation at this stage.

1 Choose **Page Setup** from the **File** menu.

2 Select the size from the **Slides sized for** field.

3 Specify the orientation required for the **Slides**.

4 Specify the orientation required for the **Notes, handouts & outline**.

5 Click **OK**.

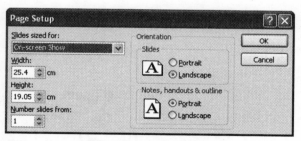

* All slides in a presentation file must be in one orientation – either landscape or portrait. If you wish to combine slides of different orientations in the same slide show, you could use hyperlinks to link separate presentation files.

The next table summarizes the main options in the **Slide sized for** list (you can check the others out in the list yourself).

Type	Width	Height	Notes
On-screen show	25.4 cm	19 cm	Orientation to Landscape; 3:4 aspect ratio
Letter paper	25.4 cm	19 cm	3:4 aspect ratio
A4 paper	27.5 cm	19 cm	Aspect ratio between that of on-screen show and 35 mm slides
35mm slides	28.5 cm	19 cm	Content will fill the slide in landscape orientation 2:3 aspect ratio
Overhead	25.4 cm	19 cm	Select for overhead transparencies
Banner	20.3 cm	2.54 cm	
Custom			Set own measurements

* If you change the slide orientation, you may find that you need to change the size and shape of placeholders on the Slide Master to get your objects to fit well.

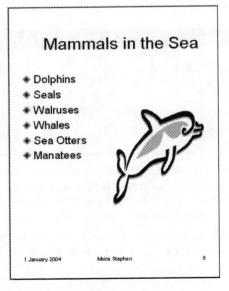

Letter paper size, portrait orientation.

11.2 Printing slides

With the Page Setup details specified for the output required, you can go ahead and print your slides. I recommend that you preview your presentation before you print it. If you do not like the preview, adjust as necessary and preview again, until you are happy that it is ready for printing.

To preview your presentation:

- Click the **Preview tool**  on the Standard toolbar, or open the **File** menu and choose **Preview**.

The Preview toolbar is displayed with your slide.

Take a look at the Preview toolbar. From left to right you have:

- **Previous Page**
- **Next Page**
- **Print...** displays the **Print** dialog box
- **Print What:** choose from slides, handouts, notes or outline
- **Zoom** – the default option fits the slide/page on the screen. You can increase or decrease it if you wish
- **Landscape** or **Portrait** – orientation options available for handouts, notes pages and outline
- **Options** – further options to choose from (see next page)
- **Close** – closes the preview window

One click printing

If you click the print icon on the Standard toolbar, one copy of each slide is printed. To print anything else you must go into Print Preview or access the **Print** dialog box and specify what to print in the **Print What:** field.

Print What:

Slides

Prints onto paper or overhead transparencies, one slide per page.

Handouts

You can print miniatures of your slides to issue as audience handouts – 1, 2, 3, 4, 6 or 9 to the page.

Printing your handouts with 3 slides to the page is particularly useful as there is room for your audience to make their own notes. The 9 slides per page option is a good way to get a summary for your own use.

Notes Pages

A slide miniature is printed, together with any notes that you have made to prompt you during your presentation.

Outline

The text of each slide is printed out, showing the structure of the presentation.

A printed outline can be very useful in that it lets you see an overview of the whole presentation.

When you choose to print handouts, notes pages or outline, the orientation tools become active so you can specify Portrait or Landscape.

Options

Other print options are available in the Options list. Some of the options are also available in the Print dialog box.

Options ▾
- Header and Footer...
- Color/Grayscale ▶
- Scale to Fit Paper
- ✓ Frame Slides
- ✓ Print Hidden Slides
- ✓ Print Comments and Ink Markup
- Printing Order ▶

Header and Footer

Displays the Header and Footer dialog box (see section 3.9).

Color/Grayscale

This option allows printing in *Color*, *Grayscale* or *Pure Black and White*. The grayscale and pure black and white options are useful for printing notes pages and handouts. The table opposite gives guidelines on how some of the objects print in grayscale and in pure black and white.

You can also choose to view your slide in grayscale or pure black and white in Normal view – the Color/Grayscale tool is on the Standard toolbar.

Object	Grayscale	Pure black and white
Text	Black	Black
Text shadows	Hidden	Hidden
Embossing	Hidden	Hidden
Fills	Grayscale	White
Frame	Black	Black
Pattern fills	Grayscale	White
Lines	Black	Black
Object shadows	Grayscale	Black
Slide backgrounds	White	White

To change the appearance of objects in Grayscale and Pure black and white in Normal View:

1 Right-click on your slide.
2 Choose **Grayscale Setting** or **Black and White Setting**.
3 Select an option.

Scale to Fit paper

This option automatically scales your slide to fit the paper size.

Frame Slides

Toggles a slide border, or frame, on or off.

Print Hidden Slides

Prints slides that have been marked as Hidden (see section 9.1) as well as those that have not.

Print Comments and Ink Markup

Prints out the comments sheet for any slide that has a comment on it, and any pen annotations retained from a slide show.

Using a service bureau

If you are going to send your slides to a service bureau to be turned into 35 mm slides or other materials, contact the bureau for any specific information on file formats required.

Print Order

Allows you to specify whether the slides are printed down the page then across, or across the page then down (handouts).

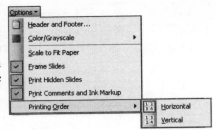

11.3 Print dialog box

Many of the options that can be specified in Print Preview, can also be specified in the **Print** dialog box.

You can display the **Print** dialog box by using **File > Print**, or by clicking Print... on the Print Preview toolbar.

Print selected slides

If you don't want to print out all of your slides, you can specify which ones you do want in either Slide Sorter view or in the Print dialog box.

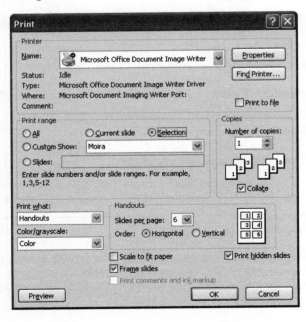

To print selected slides from Slide Sorter view:

1 Select the slides you wish to print in Slide Sorter view (click on the first one, then [Ctrl]-click on each additional slide).

2 Open the **File** menu and choose **Print...**

3 Choose **Selection**.

To select slides in the Print dialog box:

1 Display the **Print** dialog box.

2 Select **Slides** in the Print range options.

3 Enter the slide numbers required e.g. 1, 3, 5, 7-9, 15.

4 Click **OK**.

Print custom show

If you have set up custom shows (see section 9.8), you can opt to print the slide range from the custom show.

1 Display the **Print** dialog box.

2 Select **Custom Show** in the Print range options.

3 Select the show required.

4 Click **OK**.

Summary

This chapter has introduced some of the printing facilities that are available in PowerPoint. Areas covered were:

• Page Setup options for slides, notes, handouts and outline

• The Print Preview tools and printing options

• The Print dialog box

• Printing selected slides – from Slide Sorter view and from the Print dialog box

• Printing a custom show

12
jumps and links

In this chapter you will learn:

- how to use Action Buttons
- how to add text and sound
- how to combine landscape and portrait slides
- how to add a hyperlink to an object

Aims of this chapter

In this chapter we will look at Action Buttons. These are found in the AutoShapes list on the Drawing toolbar. You can use them to jump from one place to another in a presentation, or to link through to another presentation, file or program. The Action Buttons can be added to any slide you wish – they become activated when you are running your slide show on a computer.

12.1 Action Buttons and hyperlinks

A *hyperlink* is a 'hot spot' that acts as a connection to a destination within the file, in another presentation file, or to any other file or location on your network or intranet, or to a page on the Web.

The hyperlink may be text, or any other object, e.g. WordArt, graphic, chart, etc.

An *Action Button* is a ready-made hyperlink that you can insert into your presentation and edit as required.

To add an Action Button to a slide:

1 Display the slide on which you want to put an Action Button.

2 Choose **Action Buttons** from the **AutoShapes** list.

3 Select a button.

4 Click where you want the button to appear.

5 Complete the **Action Settings** dialog box.

6 Click **OK**.

7 Resize or reposition the Action Button if necessary.

- If you like adding Action Buttons to your slides, make the **Action Buttons** submenu a floating menu (drag its title bar) – to give you quick access to all the buttons. You can dock the menu at the top, bottom, right or left of your screen.

The Action Buttons toolbar

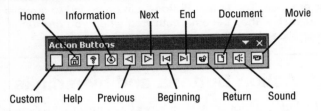

Home   Information   Next   End   Document   Movie

Custom   Help   Previous   Beginning   Return   Sound

Action Button settings

Most of the Action Buttons have default settings – and these can be easily changed in the Action Settings dialog box.

To edit the settings of an existing Action Button:

1 Right-click on the button.
2 Choose **Action Settings…** from the shortcut menu.
3 Select the **Mouse Click** or **Mouse Over** tab.
4 Specify the settings required.
5 Click **OK**.

Adding sound to your Action Button

You could add a sound to your Action Button – the sound will play when the Action Button is clicked, or when the mouse moves over it.

To add sound to an Action Button:

1 Right-click on the button.
2 Choose **Action Settings…** from the shortcut menu.
3 Select the **Mouse Click** or **Mouse Over** tab.
4 Click the **Play Sound** checkbox.
5 Select a sound from the list available.

Or

6 Click **Other sound ...** at the bottom of the list.

7 Browse through your folders until you find more sound files (there are several in C:\ Windows\Media).

8 Select the file required in the **Add Sound** dialog box.

9 Click **OK**.

10 Click **OK** at the **Action Settings** dialog box.

You can add text to any Action Button, although it is probably most likely that you will add text to the Custom button as it contains no image.

To add text to an Action Button:

1 Right-click on the button.

2 Select **Add text** from the menu.

3 Enter the text into the text box.

4 Click anywhere on your slide.

◆ Action buttons are activated when you give a slide show.

12.2 Editing buttons and hyperlinks

To change the destination of a hyperlink:

1 Select the Action Button/hyperlink on your slide.

2 Click the **Insert Hyperlink** tool ▨ .

3 Adjust the settings as required.

4 Click **OK**.

To delete an Action Button:

1 Select the Action Button.

2 Press [Delete].

To change the hyperlink text:

1 Select the text.

2 Type the new text.

To remove a hyperlink from an object:

1 Right-click on the object.

2 Left-click on **Remove Hyperlink**.

12.3 Mixed slide orientation

In any PowerPoint file, the orientation is either landscape (the default) or portrait. You can't use different orientations in the same file. If you want a presentation with slides in both orientations, Action Buttons and hyperlinks can help. You need to set up two files – one with the orientation landscape and the other portrait – then use Action Buttons to link one presentation to the other.

To link from one presentation to another:

1 Set up the main presentation – leaving out any slides that are in the other orientation, e.g. landscape.

2 Set up a second file with the remaining slides, using the other orientation.

3 In the main file, place an Action Button on the slide before a slide from the second file – use a **Custom** button.

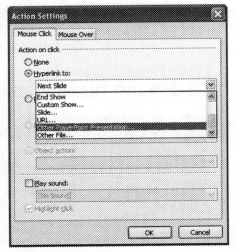

4 In **Hyperlink to:** choose **Other PowerPoint Presentation.**

5 Select the second file and click **OK.**

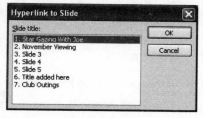

6 Specify the slide to jump to.

7 Click **OK** to close the **Hyperlink to Slide** dialog box.

8 Click **OK** to close the **Action Settings** dialog box.

To switch between files during a slide show:

1 Click the Action Button to jump to the second file when you reach the appropriate slide.

2 View the slides in the second file, using the usual techniques to move from slide to slide as necessary.

3 To return to the main presentation file, press [Esc].

12.4 Hyperlink from any object

You don't have to use Action Buttons to hyperlink to different places in your file, to another file or to an Internet address.

You can attach a hyperlink to most objects – Text, AutoShape, clip art, WordArt, etc.

To attach a hyperlink to an object:

1 Select the object you want to hyperlink from.

Or

• Place the insertion point within the word you want to hyperlink from.

2 Click the **Insert Hyperlink** tool 📷.

3 Type the path or browse for the file you want to link to – it could be on your disk, on your company intranet or on the Internet.

4 Click **OK.**

• During a slide show, you can jump to the hyperlink using your chosen method – either *Mouse Click* or *Mouse Over.*

• When you jump to a hyperlinked file, click the **Back** tool on the Web toolbar to return to your presentation.

Summary

In this chapter we have discussed:

• Adding Action Buttons to slides
• Editing Action Buttons settings
• Adding sounds to Action Buttons
• Using Action Buttons to link presentation files to produce slide shows with mixed slide orientation
• Adding hyperlinks to objects on your slides
• Editing Action Buttons and hyperlinks

13

macros

In this chapter you will learn:

- how to create and run
  macros
- about the Visual Basic Editor
- how to edit and delete
  macros

Aims of this chapter

In this chapter we will consider how macros can help you automate your work. Macros are useful when you want to automate a *routine* that you perform regularly. In this chapter we will look at some examples where you may find macros useful. You will learn how to record, play back and edit the macros you create.

13.1 What are macros?

A macro is a set of PowerPoint commands grouped together so that you can execute them as a single command.

If you perform a task often, but cannot find a PowerPoint keyboard shortcut, or tool, that runs through the sequence you want to use, you should record the commands into a macro. You have then created a 'custom' command.

What could you use a macro for?

• Speeding up routine editing and formatting.

• Recording the instructions to create a new presentation using one of your own templates.

• Quickly accessing an option in a dialog box that you regularly use.

• Combining a group of commands you often execute in the same sequence.

There are two ways to create macros in PowerPoint:

1 **Macro Recorder** – we will be using this option. You can use the Macro Recorder to record any function that you can access through the menus and dialog boxes.

2 **Visual Basic Editor** – you can create powerful, flexible macros using this. These macros can include Visual Basic commands as well as PowerPoint commands. We will take a brief excursion into the Editor when we discuss editing macros.

Macro security

Macros are potentially dangerous, and can contain viruses. For this reason there is security built into PowerPoint for the running of macros. If you create macros, then cannot run them, it is either because you are not identified as a trusted source, and/or you have not digitally signed your macros. You will find instructions on how to become a trusted source, create a digital certificate, and adjust your security levels in the Help system. If you log into a network, you may not have permissions to create and run macros at all.

13.2 Record a macro

Before you start recording your macro, think through what it is that you want to record. If there are any commands that you're not sure about, try them out first to check that they do what you want to record. This macro will record instructions that changes slide orientation from landscape to *portrait*.

To record the macro:

1 Open the **Tools** menu, choose **Macro** then **Record New Macro...**

2 Give your macro a name, e.g *Portrait*.

♦ Macro names must start with a letter and may not include spaces or most of the punctuation characters. If you want to separate words, use the underline character.

3 Select the location that you want to store the macro in.

4 Edit the **Description** if you wish.

5 Click **OK**.

♦ You will be returned to the presentation, and the Stop Recording toolbar will be displayed.

6 Work through the steps that you want to record.

7 Click the **Stop** tool on the Stop Recording toolbar when you've finished.

13.3 Run a macro

To play back your macro from the Tools menu:

1 Open the **Tools** menu and choose **Macro**.

2 Select **Macros...**

3 At the **Macros** dialog box, select the macro you want to play back and click **Run**.

♦ To assign your macro to a tool on a toolbar, see section 14.7.

13.4 Edit a macro

The macros that you record through the Macro Recorder are translated into Visual Basic – so things may look a bit strange when you first try editing a macro. But don't worry, if you take your time and have a look through the instructions you'll soon be able to relate your actions in PowerPoint to the Visual Basic code.

When editing a macro, be very careful not to delete anything you don't understand, or insert anything that should not be there – you might find your macro no longer runs properly if you do.

If the worst comes to the worst and the macro stops working, you can always record it again.

When you look through the Visual Basic code there are often far more lines of code than commands you recorded through the Macro Recorder – some instructions are picked up from default settings in dialog boxes. Just scroll through until you see something you recognize as the line you want to change.

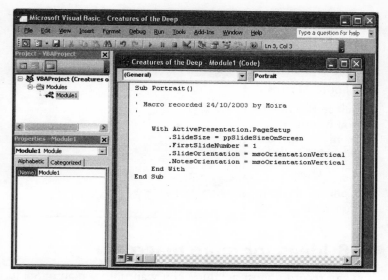

To edit a macro:

1 Open the **Tools** menu, choose **Macro** then select **Macros...**

2 Select the macro you wish to edit.

3 Click the **Edit** button.

• The Visual Basic code for the selected macro will be displayed.

4 Scroll through the code until you see the area you want to change.

5 Edit as required.

6 Save the changes – click the **Save** tool on the Standard toolbar

7 Close – click the **Close** button on the Microsoft Visual Basic title bar

13.5 Delete a macro

As you experiment with setting up macros, you will inevitably end up with some that you don't want to keep. They may not prove as useful as you first thought, or they might not run properly. You can easily delete any macro you no longer require.

To delete a macro:

1 Open the **Tools** menu and select **Macro**.

2 Choose **Macros...**

3 Select the macro you want to delete from the list displayed.

4 Click **Delete**.

5 Confirm the deletion at the prompt.

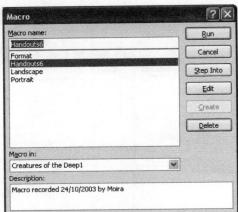

13.6 Ideas for more macros

You can record almost anything you want into a macro. Some of the things that you could record into a macro may also be automated in other ways, but as a general rule macros are used to carry out a sequence of commands.

If you find that you regularly use a series of commands in the same order, or use an option that is buried deep in a dialog box, macros can help you speed up the way you work.

Try out the macros below to get some more practice. They are all easy to set up.

Record macros that:

- Change the slide orientation back to landscape.

- Print the presentation 6 slides to the page.

- Record custom formatting to slide headings, e.g. embossed, different font, bold.

13.7 Using macros in other presentations

When you create a macro, it is stored in the presentation that you choose. The presentation must be open when you create the macro.

There will be times when you create a macro in one presentation, then wish to use it in another. When this happens you can copy the macro from one presentation to another.

1 Open the presentation that contains the macro, and the one that you want to copy it to.

2 Choose **Macros** in the **Tools** menu, then **Visual Basic Editor**.

3 In Editor on the **View** menu, click **Project Explorer**.

4 Drag the module you want to copy to the destination presentation.

Summary

In this chapter we have discussed macros. You have learnt how to:

♦ Record a macro using the Macro Recorder

♦ Run the macro

♦ Edit a macro using the Visual Basic Editor

♦ Delete a macro

♦ Copy a macro from one presentation to another

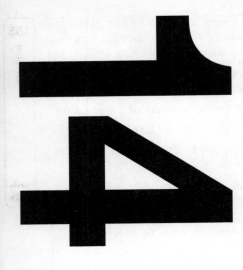

14

toolbars

In this chapter you will learn:

- how to manage toolbars
- how to add, remove and move tools on toolbars
- how to create a new toolbar
- about assigning macros to toolbars

Aims of this chapter

In this chapter we'll look at basic toolbar manipulation – the positioning of toolbars on the screen and showing and hiding toolbars. We'll also discuss how you can edit existing toolbars, create new ones and assign macros to them.

14.1 Showing and hiding toolbars

You may have noticed that some toolbars appear and disappear automatically as you work in PowerPoint. The Picture toolbar appears when a clip art object is selected, the WordArt toolbar appears when a WordArt object is selected.

You can opt to show or hide toolbars whenever you want.

Provided you have at least one toolbar displayed, you can use the shortcut method to show or hide any toolbar.

To use the shortcut method:

1 Right-click on a toolbar.

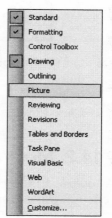

* Any toolbars that are displayed have a tick beside their name, any that are not displayed have no tick.

2 Click (using the *left* mouse button) on the toolbar name you wish to show or hide.

If no toolbars are displayed, you must use the View menu to show them again.

1 Open the View menu and choose **Toolbars**.

2 Click on the one you want to show.

Using either method, you can show or hide one toolbar at a time. If you want to change the display status of several toolbars at once, it may be quicker to use the Customize dialog box.

1 Right-click on any toolbar.

Or

* Open the View menu and choose **Toolbars**.

Or

+ Click the drop-down arrow at the right of a toolbar and choose **Add or Remove Buttons**.

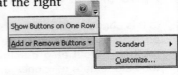

2 Click **Customize...**

3 On the **Toolbars** tab, select or deselect the toolbars as required (a tick means they are displayed, otherwise they are hidden).

4 Click **Close**.

14.2 Moving toolbars

Toolbars can be positioned *anywhere* on your screen. There are four *docking* areas – at the top, bottom, left and right of your screen, and your toolbars can be placed in any of them. You can also leave your toolbar floating in the file area if you prefer.

To move a toolbar if it is docked:

1 Point to the dotted line at the left of the toolbar (if docked at the top or bottom of the screen) or top (if docked at the left or right).

2 Drag and drop the toolbar to the position you want it in.

To move the toolbar if it is not docked:

1 Point to its Title bar.

2 Drag and drop the toolbar into its new position.

14.3 Row Sharing

The Standard and Formatting toolbars can be displayed on one row or two. You can switch the row-sharing option on or off.

1 Click the drop-down arrow to the right of the Standard or Formatting toolbar.

2 Choose **Show Buttons on One Row** or **Show Buttons on Two Rows** as required.

Or

1 Open the **Customize** dialog box – use **View > Toolbars > Customize...**

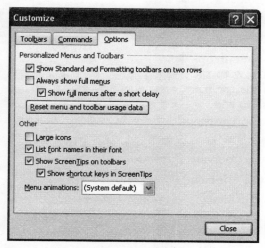

2 Display the **Options** tab.

3 Select or deselect the checkbox as required.

4 Click **Close**.

When the Standard and Formatting toolbars share one row, the toolbars are customized automatically to display the tools that you have used most recently.

To access a tool that is not displayed on the toolbar:

1 Click the drop-down arrow at the right edge of the toolbar.

2 Select the tool required from those displayed.

• The tool will be placed on the displayed area of the toolbar so that you can access it again quickly.

14.4 Editing existing toolbars

When you first start to use PowerPoint, the toolbars display the tools that perform some of the most regularly used functions, e.g. new, open, save, print.

If there are some tools on a toolbar that you tend not to use, or if you want to add another, you can easily do so. If you want to add several tools, create a new toolbar and add to that – see section 14.6.

To edit a toolbar it must be displayed.

To add or remove tools:

1 Click the drop-down arrow to the right of the toolbar you wish to edit.

2 Click **Add or Remove** buttons.

3 Choose the toolbar.

4 Select the tool to add to the toolbar.

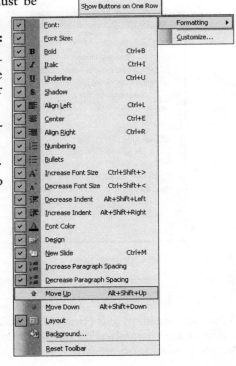

Or

♦ Deselect the tool you wish to remove.

5 Click in the presentation.

To edit an existing toolbar from the Customize dialog box:

1 Right-click on a toolbar that is currently displayed.

Or

♦ Open the **View** menu and choose **Toolbars**.

Or

♦ Click the drop-down arrow at the right of a toolbar and choose **Add or Remove Buttons**.

2 Click **Customize...**

3 Select the **Commands** tab.

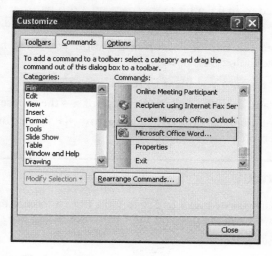

To add a tool:

1 Select the **Category** of tool you're looking for.

2 Locate the command you require from the **Commands:** list.

3 Drag it over to the toolbar. When you are over a toolbar a very dark I-beam with a **+** beside it indicates your position. Drop it in the position required (if you are not over a toolbar, the mouse pointer has a small button with an **x**).

You can move, delete and resize tools on a toolbar when the Customize dialog box is open.

To move a tool:

1 Drag the tool to its new position on the toolbar.

2 Drop it.

To remove a tool:

1 Drag the tool off the toolbar.

2 Drop it anywhere.

♦ Click **Close** when you've finished editing your toolbar.

The drop-down lists that appear on toolbars, e.g. Style box and Font box on the Formatting toolbars take up a lot more room than one of the picture tools.

If you need to make a bit more space on a toolbar that contains drop-down tools, you can change their size as required.

To change the size of a drop-down tool, you must have the **Customize** dialog box open.

1 Select the tool you want to resize, e.g. Arial

2 Click and drag the right or left edge of it – the mouse pointer becomes a thick double-headed arrow ↔ when you are in the correct place

---

Shortcut

You can quickly move or delete tools from a toolbar that is displayed *without* opening the Customize dialog box.

To move a tool:

Hold down [Alt] and drag the tool along the toolbar (or to another toolbar).

To delete a tool:

Hold down [Alt] and drag the tool off the toolbar.

14.5 Reset toolbar

If you have edited a PowerPoint toolbar, then decide that you want to reset it, you can easily do so. The toolbar will return to how it was when you installed PowerPoint.

To reset your toolbar:

1 Open the **Customize** dialog box.
2 Display the **Toolbars** tab.
3 Select the toolbar you wish to reset.
4 Click the **Reset...** button.
5 Click **OK** at the prompt.

14.6 Creating a new toolbar

If you want to add several tools to a toolbar, you may find that you need to create a new toolbar, rather than try to squeeze tools into the existing ones.

To create a new toolbar:

1 Right-click on a toolbar that is currently displayed.

Or

◆ Open the **View** menu and choose **Toolbars**.

Or

◆ Click the drop-down arrow at the right of a toolbar and choose **Add or Remove Buttons**.

2 Click **Customize...**
3 Select the **Toolbars** tab.
4 Click **New...**
5 Give your toolbar a name and click **OK**.

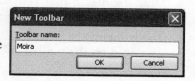

6 Your new toolbar will be displayed.

7 Choose the **Commands** tab and add the tools you require.

8 Close the **Customize** dialog box.

14.7 Assign macro to a tool

In Chapter 13 you found out how to record, run, edit and delete macros. If you use macros, it can be much more efficient to run them from a tool on a toolbar than through the Tools menu.

To assign a macro to a tool:

• The toolbar that you want to add your macro to must be displayed.

1 Display the **Customize** dialog box – **View > Toolbars > Customize**.

2 Select the **Commands** tab.

3 Scroll through the category list, and select **Macros**.

4 Drag the macro that you want to assign to a tool onto the toolbar.

• The name of the macro will be displayed on the toolbar.

Button image

You can display an image on your macro button.

To modify the appearance of a tool:

1 Select the tool.

2 Click **Modify Selection**.

3 Select **Default Style** – this displays a button image rather than text.

4 Click **Change Button Image**.

5 Choose an image from those available.

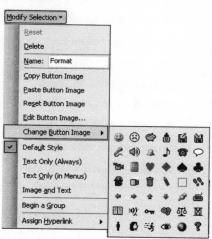

If you feel that the button images supplied are a bit meaningless for your macros, you can easily edit them.

1 Select the button you wish to modify on your toolbar.

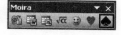

2 Click **Modify Selection**, and choose **Edit Button Image...**

3 Use the Colors and Erase options to create your own image.

4 Click **OK**.

♦ Experiment with the Modify Selection options.

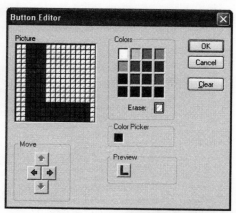

5 Close the **Customize** dialog box.

Summary

In this chapter we have discussed the various options available when working with and modifying toolbars:

+ Showing and hiding toolbars

+ Positioning toolbars on your screen

+ Row sharing

+ Adding tools to toolbars

+ Moving tools on toolbars

+ Removing tools from toolbars

+ Creating new toolbars

+ Assigning macros to tools

15

powerpoint with other applications

In this chapter you will learn:
- what linking and embedding mean
- how to use PowerPoint with Excel
- about PowerPoint presentations and Word documents

Aims of this chapter

PowerPoint is part of the Microsoft Office suite, and it integrates very well with the other applications in the suite. If you have installed the complete Office suite then you have the benefit of being able to use the best tool for the job. This chapter discusses some of the ways in which the Office applications can be integrated.

15.1 Linking vs embedding

Linking and *embedding* are two techniques that enable you to incorporate data from other applications into your PowerPoint document.

The main difference between linked and embedded data lie in:

* Where it is stored
* How it is updated.

Linked data

Linked data is not stored in your PowerPoint presentation. It is stored in a file, e.g. a workbook or document, in the source application (the one it was created in). The data is updated within the source application – and those changes are reflected in the PowerPoint presentation to which it is linked.

Features of linked data include:

* The PowerPoint presentation is smaller than it otherwise would have been.
* The data in the presentation reflects the current status of the source data.

Embedded data

Embedded data is stored in your PowerPoint presentation. However, when you create and edit the data, you have access to all the functions within the source application.

Features of embedded data:

- All the data is held in one file.

- You have access to powerful functions that are not part of PowerPoint when creating and editing the object.

The following sections discuss some of the methods you can use to integrate the data across the applications in Office.

- Section 15.2 discusses simple copy and paste techniques to get data from one application to another.

- Section 15.3 discusses Paste Special (this option enables you to link the data in one application to another).

- Section 15.4 discusses converting Word documents to PowerPoint presentations, and vice versa.

15.2 Copy and paste

You can copy text, data, graphics, charts, etc. from one application to another within the Office suite using simple copy and paste techniques.

To copy and paste:

1 Launch PowerPoint and the application you want to copy from.

2 Select the object, text or data you want to copy.

3 Click the **Copy** tool on the Standard toolbar.

4 Switch to PowerPoint and display the slide you want to paste on to.

5 Place the insertion point where you want the object, text or data to appear.

6 Click the **Paste** tool on the Standard toolbar.

Data pasted in from Excel or Access is displayed in a PowerPoint table and can be edited and formatted using PowerPoint's table-handling features. Text copied from Word is placed in a text box.

When you copy data using this method, it is not linked to the original data in Excel, Access or Word in any way. Should you edit the data in the source application, the data you copied into PowerPoint remains as it was when you copied it.

15.3 Copy and Paste Special

If you want the data that you copy into your PowerPoint document to be kept in line with the data held in the source application, you should create a link to it. You must use Copy and Paste Special to do this.

You can use Paste Special to link to files in Excel or PowerPoint.

To create a link to data or a chart in Excel:

1 Open the workbook that contains the data or chart you want to create a link to.

2 Select the data or chart required.

3 Click the **Copy** tool.

4 Switch to PowerPoint.

5 Open the presentation, and display the slide that you want to paste into.

6 Open the **Edit** menu and choose **Paste Special...**

7 Select the **Paste Link** button.

8 Choose an option from the **As:** list – when you select an option a brief description of how it works appears in the **Result** box.

9 Click **OK**.

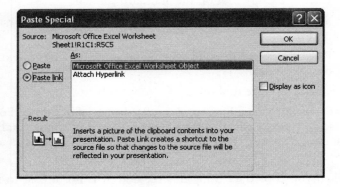

15.4 PowerPoint and Word

In addition to Copy and Paste or Paste Special techniques, there are other ways of working between PowerPoint and Word.

PowerPoint presentation from Word documents

You can quickly create a PowerPoint presentation from a Word document. The Word document must be set up as an outline (see Word online Help), and you must format the text in your Word document using the heading styles 1–9 as PowerPoint uses the heading levels to structure the slides it creates. Text formatted using the *Heading 1* style in your Word document will be used for the slide title on each new slide, *Heading 2* styles will be used as the first level of bullet points, and so on.

To create the presentation:

1 Open your Word document if necessary.

2 Choose **Send To** from the **File** menu.

3 Click **Microsoft PowerPoint**.

Word documents from PowerPoint presentations

You can also quickly generate a Word document from a PowerPoint presentation.

1 Open the presentation you want to create a document from.

2 Choose **Send To** from the **File** menu.

3 Select **Microsoft Word**.

4 Choose a page layout and paste option.

5 Click **OK**.

This is a useful option for printing two slide miniatures with speaker's notes on one page

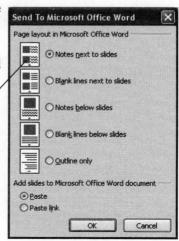

A new document will be created in Word. You can save and/or print the document as required.

If you select the Paste link option, your Word document will be automatically updated when the PowerPoint presentation is edited and saved.

Summary

In this chapter we have discussed some of the ways you can integrate PowerPoint with the rest of the Microsoft Office suite. We have discussed:

- Linking and embedding

- Copy and paste

- Copy and Paste Special from Excel and Access

- Creating a PowerPoint presentation from a Word document

- Creating a Word document from a PowerPoint presentation

If you've mastered half of what's in this book, you are well on the way to becoming a proficient PowerPoint user. If you are getting to grips with most of it, you are doing very well indeed.

You'll find lots of information on PowerPoint on the Internet, in addition to the Help option **Microsoft Office Online** that takes you to **http://office.microsoft.com/home/default.aspx**

You could also try searching the Web for sites that provide information on PowerPoint. Try entering "*Microsoft PowerPoint*" + "*Software Reviews*" into your search engine. You should come up with several sites worth a look.

If you would like to join a course to consolidate your skills, you could try your local college, or search the Internet for on-line courses. You have to pay for most courses, but you may find a free one – try searching for *+PowerPoint +Tutorial +Free*.

Good PowerPoint skills are useful on many different levels – personal, educational and vocational. Now that you have improved your PowerPoint skills, why not consider going for certification? The challenge of an exam can be fun, and a recognized certificate may improve your job prospects. There are a number of different bodies that you could consider, such as Microsoft Office Specialist or the ECDL (European Computer Driving Licence) certification. Or, if you feel more ambitious, how about other Microsoft Certified Professional exams?

Visit **http://www.microsoft.com/traincert/mcp/mous/** for more information on MOS certification or **http://www.ecdl.com** for information on ECDL.

| teach yourself | **Excel 2003**
moira stephen |

- Are you new to Excel?
- Do you want help with many of the topics commonly found in exams?
- Do you need lots of practice and examples to brush up your skills?

Excel 2003 is a comprehensive guide to this popular package which is suitable for all beginners. It progresses steadily from basic skills to more advanced features and includes time-saving shortcuts and practical advice.

Moira Stephen is a college lecturer and trainer, specializing in PC applications, and the author of numerous computing books.

teach
yourself

the internet
mac bride

- Are you keen to explore the internet with confidence?
- Do you want to get the latest news and information?
- Do you need to do business or go shopping online?

The Internet is a clear, jargon-free introduciton for anyone who wants to understand the internet and explore its rich potential. This book will help you to explore the world wide web, communicate via e-mail, find the information you need, shop or play games online and set up your own home page.

Mac Bride is an IT consultant who has written many top-selling computer programming and applications books.

teach yourself

html: publishing on the www
mac bride

- Are you an internet user?
- Do you want to move from browsing to publishing?
- Do you want to explore the possibilities of HTML?

HTML: Publishing on the WWW takes the mystery out of the technical issues and jargon of web site building. It covers the whole of HTML, from the very basics through to style sheets, clearly explained and with worked examples throughout. With this book you can learn enough to create a colourful, illustrated web page in just a few hours, or put together a full-featured, interactive, interlinked web site in a few days.

Mac Bride is an IT consultant who has written many top-selling computer programming and applications books.

teach yourself	**C++** richard riley

- Are you new to programming?
- Do you need to improve your existing C++ skills?
- Do you want to become an expert programmer?

C++ is a concise guide to programming in C++, one of the most popular and versatile languages in use today. All the concepts and techniques you need to create powerful programs are clearly explained with examples and revision exercises used throughout.

Richard Riley is a computer programmer who has written extensively in C++, Perl, Java, Javascript and HTML.

teach yourself

QuarkXpress
christopher lumgair

- Do you need a basic introduction to QuarkXPress?
- Do you want help to create more attractive documents?
- Do you need to brush up your QuarkXPress skills?

QuarkXPress introduces you to the essentials of the program, guiding you through the text entry, page layout and production processes in easy-to-follow stages. By concentrating on techniques, the book will enable you to create well-crafted, professional-looking documents with the minimum of effort.

Christopher Lumgair has a BA in Graphic Design and has spent several years working in both magazine and book publishing. He now runs his own successful digital publishing consultancy.